# Collins

## INTERNATIONAL PRIMARY ENGLISH

## Student's Book 4

William Collins' dream of knowledge for all began with the publication of his first book in 1819. A self-educated mill worker, he not only enriched millions of lives, but also founded a flourishing publishing house. Today, staying true to this spirit, Collins books are packed with inspiration, innovation and practical expertise. They place you at the centre of a world of possibility and give you exactly what you need to explore it.

Collins. Freedom to teach.

Published by Collins
An imprint of HarperCollins*Publishers*
The News Building
1 London Bridge Street
London SE1 9GF

Macken House, 39/40 Mayor Street Upper, Dublin 1, D01 C9W8, Ireland

Browse the complete Collins catalogue at
www.collins.co.uk

© HarperCollins*Publishers* Limited 2021

10 9 8 7 6

ISBN 978-0-00-836766-4

All rights reserved. No part of this publication may be reproduced, stored in a retrieval system, or transmitted in any form by any means, electronic, mechanical, photocopying, recording or otherwise, without the prior written permission of the Publisher or a licence permitting restricted copying in the United Kingdom issued by the Copyright Licensing Agency Ltd, 5th Floor, Shackleton House, 4 Battle Bridge Lane, London SE1 2HX.

British Library Cataloguing-in-Publication Data
A catalogue record for this publication is available from the British Library.

Authors: Catherine Baker and Daphne Paizee
Series editor: Daphne Paizee
Publisher: Elaine Higgleton
Product developer: Natasha Paul
Project manager: Karen Williams
Development editor: Sonya Newland
Copyeditor: Karen Williams
Proofreader: Catherine Dakin
Cover designer: Gordon MacGilp
Cover illustrator: Richard Johnson
Internal designer and typesetter: Ken Vail Graphic Design Ltd.
Text permissions researcher: Rachel Thorne
Image permissions researcher: Alison Prior
Illustrators: Ken Vail Graphic Design Ltd., Advocate Art, Beehive Illustration and QBS Learning
Production controller: Lyndsey Rogers
Printed and bound in India by Replika Press Pvt. Ltd.

Third-party websites, publications and resources referred to in this publication have not been endorsed by Cambridge Assessment International Education.

With thanks to the following teachers and schools for reviewing materials in development: Amanda DuPratt, Shreyaa Dutta Gupta, Sharmila Majumdar, Sushmita Ray and Sukanya Singhal, Calcutta International School; Akash Raut, DSB International School, Mumbai; Melissa Brobst, International School of Budapest; Shalini Reddy, Manthan International School; Taman Rama Intercultural School.

This book contains FSC™ certified paper and other controlled sources to ensure responsible forest management.

For more information visit: www.harpercollins.co.uk/green

# Contents

**How to use this book**

1 **Stories of the past**  page 1

2 **Mars: the trip of a lifetime!**  page 13

3 **The power of the sea**  page 26

4 **Other people, other places**  page 39

5 **The only problem is …**  page 51

6 **Making the headlines**  page 63

7 **Inventions**  page 75

8 **Putting on a show**  page 87

9 **Imaginary worlds**  page 97

## To the teacher

# How to use this book

- **Key texts and images**
  The texts in Stage 4 provide a wide variety of different genres for learners to enjoy. The colourful illustrations provide enjoyment as well as essential support for the learners as they read. Learners will read stories by published authors and are introduced to variety of different illustration styles and images.

- **Remember boxes**
  These are used to remind learners to do things that they have already learned, such as the correct use of punctuation marks.

  > **Remember!**
  > You can change the beginning or ending of a story to make your own version. You can also change the characters or the setting.

- **Spelling log**
  These are used throughout this course. Spelling logs allow learners to compile their own personal dictionaries which they can refer to in their writing activities. They also help learners to develop dictionary skills.

  > **Spelling log**
  > Record powerful verbs in your spelling log and try to use them in your own writing.

- **Thinking time**
  These occur at the end of each unit in the Student's Book. Learners are encouraged to reflect on what they have read, listened to, discussed and learned.

  > **Thinking time**
  > Do you think you should believe everything you read in newspaper and magazine articles? What could you do to check?

# 1 Stories of the past

## Listening and speaking

**1** Listen as your teacher tells you about the 'Ragged Schools'.

**2** PAIR WORK. If you were a poor child in Britain 150 years ago, would you have wanted to go to a Ragged School? Give a reason for your answer.

**3** Look at the pictures and talk about the questions.

  a  What is going on in the picture of the Ragged School?
  b  What do you think the children in the Ragged School are learning about?
  c  How is the Ragged School different from a modern primary school?
  d  How might the two schools be similar?
  e  Which sort of school would you rather go to? Give a reason.

## Reading and writing

**1** Your teacher will read you a text from a story called *Street Child*. First read the introduction and background below. What is the story about?

> *Street Child* is based on the true story of Jim Jarvis. One of the main characters is Doctor Thomas Barnardo (Barnie), who set up a Ragged School and a home for street children. He also set up a charity for children (called Barnardo's) which still exists today.
>
> The **setting** of the story is London in the 1860s. Jim Jarvis has nowhere to live. He finds a warm welcome at Doctor Barnardo's Ragged School, but soon it is time to leave for the day.

**2** How might Jim feel when it is time to leave? What do you think will happen next? Read the story to yourself silently. You will notice that Jim does not use Standard English.

"You ought to go home at once," Barnie insisted. "Your mother will know the other boys have gone. She'll wonder what kept you so late."

"I ain't got no mother."

"Your father, then."

"I ain't got no father."

Barnie was getting impatient, Jim could see that. It was almost as if he didn't believe him. "Where are your friends, then? Where do you live?"

"Ain't got no friends. Don't live nowhere."

Barnie stared at him. He walked away from the fire and back to it again, then went to the desk. He sat down on his chair and stayed with his fingers drumming across the flat of the desk-top, like the patter of rain on a roof. Jim wondered if he was angry with him.

"It's the truth, sir," he said anxiously, "I ain't telling you no lies."

He spoke in the whiny voice the other street boys used to adults.

"Tell me," the man said at last. "How many boys are there like you? Sleeping out in the streets?"

"Heaps," said Jim. "More than I can count."

It was Barnie's turn now to stare into the fire, as if there were secrets in its flames, or answers to great puzzles. He was as still and quiet as if he had gone to sleep, and Jim kept still too, afraid to break into the man's thinking. The only sound was the spitting of the logs, and outside, the bleak voice of the wind.

"Now," the man said, very slowly, like someone creeping up on a bird in case they frightened it away. "If I am willing to give you some hot coffee and a place to sleep in, will you take me to where some of these other boys are?"

Jim looked sideways at him.

"You wouldn't tell the police?"

"No," said Barnie. "I wouldn't tell the police."

"All right," said Jim. "I'll take you."

It was some time later that they arrived at the high wall of the market. Jim stopped, afraid again. What if Barnie told the police about them, and sent all the boys to the workhouse? But if he didn't show Barnie, he wouldn't get the hot meal and the shelter to sleep in. He didn't know what to do.

from *Street Child* by Berlie Doherty

**3  PAIR WORK. Talk about the questions. Then write down the answers.**

a  Describe the setting in your own words. Make your description as detailed as possible, so a reader can really imagine it.

b  Why do you think Barnie wants Jim to show him some of the other boys who sleep on the streets?

c  Why is Jim so worried that Barnie might tell the police?

d  What are the advantages and disadvantages for Jim, if he takes Barnie to see the other boys?

e  Do you think Jim will decide to take Barnie to meet the other boys? Why, or why not?

f  Is this text fiction or non-fiction?

# Reading and writing

**1** Read the information in the box.

## Dialect

Jim doesn't use standard English – he speaks in a dialect. He uses the phrase 'I ain't' instead of 'I have not' and 'I am not'. He also says 'no' instead of 'any'. So when Jim says, "Ain't got no friends", in standard English we would say, "I haven't got any friends".

**2** Write out Jim's sentences below in standard English. Change the 'ain't's and 'no's so the sentences are correct.

a "I ain't got no mother."
b "I ain't got no father."
c "I ain't telling you no lies."

### Thinking deeper

Role-play a scene in which two characters use non-standard English to speak to each other.

## Using powerful verbs

**1** Write out the sentences below. Underline the powerful verbs.

   a "You ought to go home at once," Barnie insisted.
   b Barnie stared at him.
   c The only sound was the spitting of the logs.
   d Barnie spoke very slowly, like someone creeping up on a bird.

**2** Write out the sentences below. Change the underlined verbs into more powerful ones.

   a Barnie <u>went</u> away from the fire.
   b "All right," <u>said</u> Jim.
   c Jim <u>stopped</u>, afraid again.
   d Barnie <u>looked</u> at the fire.

### Powerful verbs

Powerful verbs are verbs which help the reader imagine what is happening. For example, in this sentence, the powerful verb is 'strode': 'The teacher strode across the classroom.'

You can often use a powerful verb instead of a weaker, boring verb. For example instead of 'said', you could use 'exclaimed' or 'muttered' or 'snarled'.

### Spelling log

Record powerful verbs in your spelling log and try to use them in your own writing.

## Punctuation

**1** Look for sentences in the story that contain the punctuation marks below.

   a A sentence ending in a question mark.
   b A sentence ending in a full stop.
   c A sentence with speech marks.
   d A sentence with an apostrophe that shows possession (e.g. Tom's house; the girl's shoe; the cat's bowl).
   e A sentence with one comma.
   f A sentence with two commas.

**2** Write the sentences you have found in the story. Include all the punctuation marks.

**3** How do the commas help the reader to understand these sentences?

## Spelling and vocabulary

**1** **The sentence below from the story has a verb with double consonants.**

'He sat down on his chair and stayed with his fingers <u>drumming</u> across the flat of the desk-top.'

**a** Find two other sentences from the story that have verbs with double consonants before *–ing* or *–ed*. Write out the sentences and underline the verbs.

**b** Add *–ing* to each of these verbs. Use the rules above to help you work out whether you need to double the consonant or not.

- hop
- swim
- wait
- hoot
- sit
- patter
- dig

> ### Verbs with double consonants
> When you add a suffix like *–ed* or *–ing* to some verbs that end with a consonant (like 'stop' or 'fit'), you need to double the consonant at the end.
>
> For example:  stop   stopped   stopping
>                       fit   fitted   fitting
>
> But be careful! You don't double the last consonant if the verb:
> - ends with two consonants, like 'walk'
>   walk   walked   walking
> - has more than one syllable, like 'list/en'
>   listen   listened   listening
> - has a long vowel sound, like 'float'
>   float   floated   floating

**2** **The underlined verbs in the sentences below are spelled wrongly. Write out the sentences correctly.**

**a** Ahmed is <u>puting</u> his socks on.
**b** I love <u>eatting</u> pizza.
**c** Leena <u>waitted</u> a long time for her brother.
**d** Miguel's new top <u>fited</u> him perfectly.

### Spelling log

Add some verbs with double consonants to your spelling log.

## Reading: comprehension

**PAIR WORK. Take turns to read this diary entry out loud.**

## Ebenezer Grimes's diary

### 23 November 1870

Dear Diary,

Today I met the most extraordinary man! His name is Dr Thomas Barnardo. I was dining this evening at my friend Robert Grimshaw's house, and Dr Barnardo was also among the guests. After the meal, I found myself seated next to Dr Barnardo, and we had a very interesting conversation as we drank our coffee.

Dr Barnardo dedicates all of his energy and time to the excellent cause of helping London's street children. His Ragged School in the East End of London has been educating destitute children for the last three years, but he has also recently opened a Home for destitute boys. He provides a warm, safe bed as well as food and clothing for some of London's poorest boys, because they have nowhere else to go. However, he does not merely wait for destitute boys to come to him. He often goes out into the dangerous slum areas of the East End of our city, so that he can find children in desperate need of a home.

At first, he told me, he was keen to avoid taking in too many boys. However, one tragic night, a boy named John Somers came looking for a bed, but the Home was full that night. Dr Barnardo therefore sent John, who was known as Carrots, away. Barnardo later learnt that Carrots died just two days later, of hunger and cold. Therefore, since that fateful occasion, Dr Barnardo has never turned another child away. The motto above the door of his home is now 'No Destitute Child Ever Refused Admission'.

I returned home this evening tired, but inspired and full of determination. I will tell all my friends about Dr Barnardo's important work. I will also do all that I can to raise money to help him continue to look after the destitute children in his care.

Ebenezer Grimes

## Comprehension

**GROUP WORK. Talk about the questions. Then write the answers.**

a Who is the writer of this diary entry? Which city does he live in?

b What features of a diary entry can you see in this text?

c Find and copy one sentence that is in the present tense, one that is in the past tense and one that is in the future tense. Underline the verbs.

d Name two ways in which Dr Barnardo helped poor children, according to the diary.

e Using clues from the text, work out what 'destitute' means and write a definition.

f In your own words, explain how meeting John Somers changed things for Dr Barnardo.

g What effect did meeting Dr Barnardo have on the writer of the diary?

h Compare the diary entry with the story on pages 2–3. Which is most effective in giving information? Which helps you imagine the scene more clearly? Which do you prefer? Give reasons for your answers and refer back to the texts.

i Write one sentence to sum up the main message of this diary entry.

### Check!

You can find diaries in the library under the number 920, according to the Dewey classification system.

### Diaries

Diaries are personal stories about events in our lives. People write about their thoughts, feelings and experiences in diaries. They also write about hopes and plans for the future.

Diaries:
- are non-fiction.
- often have days or dates.
- sometimes have names.
- use personal pronouns such as 'I', 'me' and 'my'.
- are written in the past tense if they are about something that happened.
- can be written in the future tense if they are about hopes or plans for the future.

# Using adjectives and connectives

## Adjectives

Adjectives describe nouns. For example, in the sentence 'It was a hot day,' the adjective 'hot' tells us *what kind of* day it was.

Sometimes we use adjectives to show different amounts or degrees of the same thing. For example, try swapping 'hot' in the sentence above with these adjectives:

>   mild   warm   scorching

'Mild' and 'warm' are both less strong than 'hot'. 'Scorching' is stronger than 'hot'.

**1** In the phrase 'We had a very interesting conversation', the adjective 'interesting' describes the noun 'conversation'.

- Reread the diary entry and find at least four other phrases or sentences that contain adjectives.
- Write them down and underline the adjectives.

## Spelling log

Add interesting adjectives to your spelling log.

**2** Find two similar strong adjectives in the box for each adjective.

> freezing   unusual   big
> cold   huge   elderly
> extraordinary   grown-up

a cool
b enormous
c ancient
d odd

## Connectives

Connectives are the words we use to join one part of a sentence to another, for example: 'I returned home this evening tired, <u>but</u> inspired <u>and</u> full of determination.' Both 'but' and 'and' are connectives. Other common connectives include 'because', 'or', 'although' and 'so'.

Sometimes we use connectives at the start of a sentence, to connect a whole sentence or paragraph to the previous sentence or paragraph. Look at this sentence: '<u>However</u>, he does not merely wait for destitute boys to come to him.'

**3** Find and write one sentence from the diary entry that uses each of the connectives below.

a because
b but
c and
d so
e therefore

**4** Write your own sentences using each of the connectives in question 3.

# Writing

**Plan and write your own historical story based on the diary entry about Thomas Barnardo.**

## Step 1: Planning

- Reread the diary entry and talk about it with your partner. What do you learn from the diary about Dr Barnardo and Carrots?
- Talk about your ideas with your partner.

**Make notes about:**
- where the story is set
- when the story is set
- how you can show the reader what things were like at that time
- the characters and what they are like
- how the story will start
- what problems the characters will have
- how the story will end

- Write a paragraph plan for your story.
- Use your plan to write a first draft of your story.

**A paragraph plan needs:**
- a heading to show which part of the story the paragraph is about.
- notes about the setting, characters and what happens in the paragraph.

**Remember!**

This is just a plan – it's not the whole story. Write short notes, not complete sentences.

## Step 2: Redrafting and revising

Read your first draft out loud to yourself. Look out for the following things and make corrections.
- Does the story make sense?
- Is it exciting enough?
- Does it give a good sense of what life was like at that time?
- Do all the sentences make sense? Are there any words missing, or words that don't fit the sentence?
- Have you used powerful verbs and adjectives to make your story interesting?
- Have you used connectives to link different parts of a sentence and to link one sentence to another?
- Have you got the right sort of punctuation at the end of all your sentences (. ! or ?)?
- Have you used commas to separate the different parts of your sentences?
- Are all the words spelled correctly?

## Step 3: Improving

Take turns to read your story out loud to your partner. Can they make any suggestions to improve the story?

Write a final version of your story. Include any suggestions that you think improve the story.

### Thinking time

What have you learned about children who lived in London in the past by reading stories and diary entries?

# 2 Mars: the trip of a lifetime!

**Listening, speaking and writing**

1. Write two headings: 'Good things about going to Mars' and 'Bad things about going to Mars'.

2. Listen as your teacher reads you some information about the planet Mars. Make some notes under your two headings.

3. Decide whether you would like to go to Mars or not.
   - Write down three good reasons for your decision.
   - Then use your reasons to persuade everyone else in the class.

### Remember!
When working in pairs:
- take turns.
- respond politely.
- do not interrupt.
- ask questions.

## Reading and writing

**1** Look at the advertisement below. What do you read first? Why? What parts of the advertisement look interesting?

**2** The writer of this advertisement wants to persuade you to go on a trip to Mars. Read the advertisement silently to yourself.

▶ click <u>here</u> to book your trip

# Visit Mars – for the trip of a lifetime!

Are you looking for a totally unforgettable adventure?

Are you tired of unexciting trips to the beach or the countryside?

If so, you're in luck! Join us for a glorious experience that is *really* out of this world. Put on your spacesuit and let us transfer you to Mars!

## Mars is exciting

- Be courageous and visit Olympus Mons – the biggest and best volcano in the Solar System!
- Gasp at the amazing Valles Marineris canyon – far bigger and deeper than any canyon on Earth!
- Feel the unimaginable, dangerous power of a Martian duststorm!

▶ click <u>here</u> to book your trip

## Mars is fun

- Jump in a dune buggy and race your friends across the red sand.
- See who can build the biggest sandcastle.
- Whizz across the surface of Mars in a sand yacht.
- Watch the unbeatable red and pink sunsets.
- Join the search for life on Mars!

## Mars is safe

Mars is very different from Earth, but don't worry – we'll transport you safely and make sure you're safe and happy during your visit!

Your spacesuit will give you plenty of oxygen so you won't have to breathe the deadly carbon dioxide in the air. The cosy spacesuit will also keep you warm – so you needn't worry about freezing in the −62 °C temperatures!

There's nothing to eat on Mars, but you won't go hungry! Our hi-tech, transparent spaceship carries a wide range of delicious space-snacks and drinks for you to enjoy.

## What are you waiting for?

Hurry – don't lose your place on this unmissable trip! It only costs 1000 times more than an aeroplane flight round the world – what a bargain!

③ **Skim read the text again. Then answer the questions below.**

a What is Olympus Mons?

b Which of the activities mentioned in the advertisement do you think sounds most fun? Why do you think this?

c Give two reasons why you would need a spacesuit if you went to Mars.

d Do you think the advertisement is right to say the trip is a bargain? Give a reason for your answer.

e Find a sentence that is trying to make the Mars trip sound exciting. Write out the sentence and underline the exciting words.

f Find a sentence that might make the reader want to sign up for the trip quickly. Write out the sentence.

g Find a sentence that persuades the reader that it's safe to go to Mars. Write out the sentence.

h Why do you think the advertisement starts with a question?

i What kind of person do you think would go on this trip to Mars? Write two sentences to describe them.

### Facts and opinions

Advertisements often use a mix of fact and opinion to persuade the reader.

**Facts** are things that can be proven to be true or false. For example, it's a fact that the Earth travels around the Sun and that New Delhi is the capital of India. **Opinions** are things that can't be proven and that not everyone would necessarily agree with. For example, 'chocolate cake is delicious' is an opinion and so is 'Mars is a great place for a holiday'.

### Thinking deeper

Why do you think some people want to visit places like the Moon and the planets? What would advertisements for travel to these places need to say in order to persuade people to go?

**Reading and speaking**

**GROUP WORK.** Find an advertisement that interests you. Talk about how the language tries to persuade you. Do a presentation to the class about the language.

## Using exclamations

**Write out the orders below. Add the missing exclamation marks and capital letters. Then underline the imperative verbs.**

a come with us for the experience of a lifetime
b take your feet off the table
c go to sleep at once
d shut all the doors and windows
e help me find my mobile phone
f come and play football with rajiv emma and me

### Advertisements

Persuasive texts such as adverts often contain orders. Orders are sentences that tell the reader to do something – like, 'Put on your spacesuit and come with us to Mars!' Sentences like this make the reader feel as if he or she is going to do what the advertisement is saying.

### Orders

When we write orders we begin the sentence with an imperative verb (sometimes called a 'bossy verb'!). For example:

- <u>Put</u> your coat on.
- <u>Run</u> as fast as you can – the giant's coming!
- <u>Enjoy</u> a delicious meal at Pete's Pizza Parlour!
- <u>Take off</u> that dinosaur suit at once and <u>come</u> inside for lunch!

Orders often – but not always – end in an exclamation mark.

## Spelling and vocabulary

### The prefixes un– and trans– and the suffixes –able and –ous

When you add a prefix or suffix to a word, it changes the meaning.

If you add the prefix *un–* to 'well', it becomes 'unwell'. *Trans–* is a prefix that means 'across', so 'transport' is something that carries you 'across' land, sea or air.

The suffix *–able* turns a verb like 'imagine' into the adjective 'imaginable'. The suffix *–ous* turns a noun like 'danger' into the adjective 'dangerous'.

**Answer the questions below about spelling and vocabulary in the Mars advertisement on pages 14 and 15.**

- **a** Find five words with the prefix *un–* and write them.
- **b** Find four words with the suffix *–able* and write them.
- **c** Find three words with the prefix *trans–* and three words with the suffix *–ous*. Write them.
- **d** Think of four new words using the suffixes *–ous* and *–able* and the prefixes *trans–* and *un–*. Write a sentence using each word.

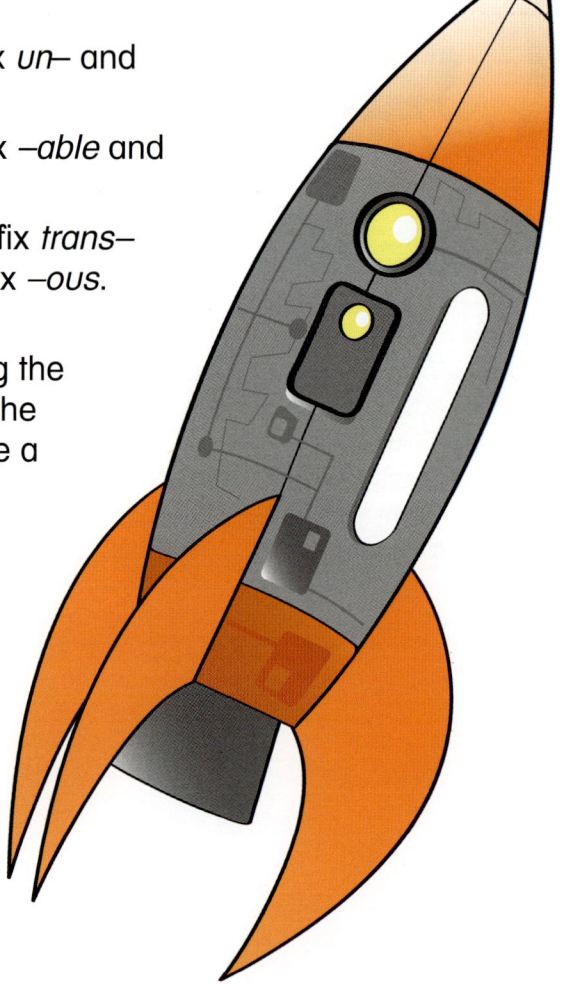

## Reading

**1** Read the advertisement below.

# Incredible Astronaut Ice Cream!

- Do you dream of travelling among the stars and zooming into space like an astronaut?
- Would you like to experience the thrill of a space walk and see our beautiful planet from high above?
- Most people aren't lucky enough to actually go into space. But now, thanks to our highly advanced freeze-drying technology, everyone can experience Astronaut Ice Cream!
- This tasty freeze-dried block of creamy goodness is like the food real astronauts eat in space. It's harder than ordinary ice cream so it won't melt, even in space! It might not transport you to the stars, but it'll make you feel on top of the world!

So don't delay – <u>buy a pack</u> today!

**2** Write the answers to the questions below.

  a  Why is the product in this advertisement called 'Astronaut Ice Cream'?
  b  'Incredible' is an adjective used to persuade the reader that the ice cream is really special. Find two other persuasive adjectives in the advertisement.
  c  In what way is this ice cream different from normal ice cream?
  d  Find one question, one order and one statement in the advertisement.
  e  PAIR WORK. Think of an interesting new type of ice cream. Work together to write an advertisement for it.

## Questions and statements

**Questions** often begin with a question word, such as 'who', 'what', 'where', 'when', 'why' or 'how'. For example:
- <u>What</u> is in this mysterious box?
- <u>Why</u> are you looking at me like that?

In **statements** the subject of the sentence usually comes before the verb. For example:
- My robot cleaned the kitchen.

    subject      verb

## Listening and speaking

**PAIR WORK.**

**1** Invent a new type of robot that can do jobs around the house. What can your robot do? If it could speak what would it sound like?

**2** Write some notes about the questions below.
- What might happen if the robot suddenly went wrong?
- What damage could he cause?
- What would he say?
- What would his owner say?

**3** Use your notes to make up a short scene between the robot and his owner.

- Use your voice and actions to make the scene funny and exciting.
- Then perform the scene for your group or class.

## Reading

**PAIR WORK.** Sometimes writers want to explain why they believe something. They try to persuade other people to believe it too. Read and talk about the text below. Has the writer persuaded you? Give a reason for your answer.

# Don't send humans to Mars!

Human beings love to explore! It's not surprising that many people want to see manned flights to Mars. After all, by sending people to Mars, we can learn more about how the planet was formed, and make all kinds of scientific discoveries. However, although the study of space is important, I believe that we should not be sending people to Mars.

Firstly, think about the cost. It is far more expensive to send people to Mars than it is to send robots, because robots don't need food and water, and if something goes wrong they don't have to be rescued. Why send humans to Mars at vast expense, when the same job can be done by robots far more cheaply?

Secondly, think about the safety issues. It takes around 15 minutes for messages to travel between Earth and Mars using radio waves – so if a terrible accident happened on a spaceship orbiting Mars, it would be impossible to respond quickly. Also, we don't yet know exactly what the effect of a very long space flight would be on the human body.

In addition, most of the science that could be done by humans on Mars can also be done by robots. This means we would not get much extra benefit for all the extra cost of sending humans rather than robots into space.

The robotic Mars Curiosity Rover does just as good a job as a human astronaut!

Finally, there are many more effective things we could spend our money on. If we want to invest in space exploration, we could put money into making a human colony or settlement on the Moon. Or we could develop space-based solar power, to help solve our energy problems on Earth. There are many other ways of spending this money too.

For all these reasons, I believe that we should not be trying to send humans to Mars – and I hope that now you are convinced of this too!

## Comprehension

**Answer the questions below.**

a  Why does the writer say it's not surprising people want to travel to Mars?

b  What does the writer think would be a better use of money than sending people to Mars?

c  Why is it cheaper to send robots to Mars than humans?

d  Give two reasons why the writer thinks it could be unsafe to send people to Mars.

e  Reread the first paragraph. Write one sentence to sum up the main point in this paragraph.

f  Think of a heading for each of the six paragraphs. Your headings should help the reader to see the main point of each paragraph.

## Using connectives

**Connectives** help the reader to see the connections between one sentence or paragraph and another. They also help us to understand a sequence of events.

Some connectives, such as 'if', 'because' and 'although', help to structure an argument by showing how ideas are connected:

- <u>Although</u> whales live under water, they are actually mammals, not fish.
- Fish cannot breathe <u>if</u> they are taken out of water.
- My favourite sea creature is the dolphin, <u>because</u> they look as if they are smiling.

Some connectives, such as 'firstly', 'next' and 'then', help to show the order or sequence of ideas and events:

- <u>Firstly</u>, I toasted two slices of bread.
- <u>Next</u>, I got the chocolate spread out of the cupboard.
- <u>Then</u> I put a thick layer of chocolate spread on the toast.

1. **Answer the questions below about connectives.**

    a   Look at *Don't send humans to Mars!* on page 21. Find and write three sentences with connectives that show the order of ideas.

    b   Find and write two sentences with connectives that show how ideas are connected.

    c   Find and write one sentence with the connective 'and'.

    d   Write a new sentence of your own using the connective 'but'.

> **Commas to mark out meaning in sentences**
>
> Commas help us to read and understand long sentences.
> - After all, by sending people to Mars, we can learn more about how the planet was formed, and make all kinds of scientific discoveries.
> - Remembering what my mother had told me, I took off my muddy boots when I came indoors, although I didn't realise my socks were muddy too, so the carpet got dirty anyway.

2. **Write out the sentences below. Add the missing commas.**

    a   After I came home from school I went straight upstairs because I wanted to see Marvin my pet gecko.

    b   It was getting late although the sun was still shining brightly and I didn't realise that it was past my bedtime.

    c   Running down the road Maria wasn't looking where she was going so she bumped into Mrs Martinez who was chatting to her friend.

## Writing

Plan and write your own persuasive text to convince the reader to visit your local area or another place that you like.

### Remember!

Think about how you will present your work and what will work best.

Will you use a computer and present the text for people to read on screen? Or would a handwritten text be better? Why?

### Step 1: Planning

**1** Decide which place you are going to write about. Will it be your local area, or somewhere else?

**2** Do some research about the place you have chosen and find as many reasons as you can why people should visit it. You could talk to local people, read books or information leaflets, or search for ideas on the internet. Make notes about:
- the history of the area.
- interesting things to see.
- fun things to do.
- any local specialities, for example, special, local food that visitors might enjoy.

**3** Use your notes to plan how you will divide your text up into paragraphs.

**4** Now use your paragraph plan to help you write your persuasive text.

# Step 2: Redrafting and revising

**5** Read your text aloud and check that it makes sense and is correct.

**6** Now show your text to a friend or partner. Do they find it convincing? Can they make any suggestions to make it even more persuasive?

**7** Write a final version of your text. You could also add some pictures or photographs.

## Thinking time

Work in groups. Read the persuasive texts that you have written. Which places would you like to visit, based on the texts?

# 3 The power of the sea

## Speaking and writing

**1** PAIR WORK. Look at the pictures below. Imagine you are standing on a cliff or beach looking out at the sea in both pictures. Talk about:

- what you can see, hear and feel.
- what you can taste and smell.
- how the sea makes you feel.

**2** Write at least two words and phrases for each bullet point above.

### Spelling log

Record the words you choose in your spelling log.

## Reading and writing

**1** PAIR WORK. Listen as your teacher reads the poems below out loud. Then read them with your partner.

# Windy Nights

Whenever the moon and stars are set,
Whenever the wind is high,
All night long in the dark and wet,
A man goes riding by.
Late in the night when the fires are out,
Why does he gallop and gallop about?

Whenever the trees are crying aloud,
And ships are tossed at sea,
By, on the highway, low and loud,
By at the gallop goes he.
By at the gallop he goes and then
By he comes back at the gallop again.

by Robert Louis Stevenson

## Sea Haiku

Like angry grey ghosts
the waves hurl handfuls of stones
against the dark shore.

## Tanka

My boat bobs gently;
sunlight tickles the wavelets,
and I sun myself
like a sleek, contented cat,
one eye half-open for fish.

**2** Write the answers to the questions below.

   a Describe the setting of the poem *Windy Nights*.
   b Write three pairs of rhyming words from the first verse of *Windy Nights*.
   c In the second verse of *Windy Nights*, what do you think the poet means when he says 'the trees are crying aloud'?
   d Why do you think the man in *Windy Nights* might be galloping about? Where could he be going and why?
   e Find a simile in *Sea Haiku* and write it out. Do you think it is an effective simile? Why, or why not?
   f Find two alliterative words (words that are close together and start with the same letter) in *Sea Haiku*.
   g Reread *Sea Haiku*. Write two sentences to describe what you might see if you were standing on the shore.
   h In *Tanka*, which animal does the poet compare herself to? Why do you think the poet chose this animal?
   i Why do you think the poet says, 'sunlight tickles the wavelets' rather than 'sunlight shines on the wavelets'?

**3** Which of the three poems do you like best and why? Write a note to a friend recommending your favourite.

### Alliteration

Writers sometimes use words that have the same beginning letters. For example:

My **b**oat **b**obs gently ...

By at the **g**allop **g**oes he ...

Alliteration helps readers focus on the sounds in a poem.

### Similes

Similes give writing more impact. Writers often use similes to compare one thing to another. Similes use the words 'like' or 'as ... as'. For example:

- The wind howled <u>like</u> a hungry wolf.
- The sunlight was <u>as</u> warm <u>as</u> melted butter.
- Mum's eyes are <u>as</u> sweet and brown <u>as</u> toffee.

## Using similes

**1** Write a simile about the weather today.

**2** Write a simile about your best friend or a member of your family.

## Reading and writing

1. Read the tanka about bare trees in the orange box. Write it out. Add capital letters and punctuation.

2. Which of these two poems do you prefer? Give a reason for your answer.

## Haiku and tanka

Haiku and tanka are both types of short poems which come from Japan. They do not rhyme. They normally describe a single moment, feeling or idea – a bit like a photograph.

**Haiku** have three lines. The first line has five syllables, the second has seven syllables and the third has five syllables, like this:

- Scatt/er/ing sun/light,
  1   2   3   4   5
- danc/ing in the frisk/y wind:
  1    2   3   4   5   6   7
- hap/py wild/flow/ers.
  1   2    3    4    5

**Tanka** have five lines. Usually the first line has five syllables, the second has seven, the third has five, the fourth has seven and the fifth has seven syllables, like this:

- the trees' bare branch/es
  1    2     3     4     5
- swish like thick ropes of sea/weed
  1     2     3    4    5   6    7
- this rain-lashed gar/den
  1     2      3     4    5
- hun/dreds of miles from the sea
  1    2    3   4    5    6   7
- is sud/den/ly an o/cean
  1   2   3   4  5  6   7

Sometimes haiku and tanka have normal sentence punctuation (with capital letters, commas, full stops and so on) and sometimes they don't. It's up to the poet.

## Using verbs and adjectives

Poems often contain powerful descriptive words that help to create a strong mood or feeling. Answer the questions below about the poems.

a Find and write a powerful verb from *Windy Nights*. Can you think of another verb that means the same?

b Find two adjectives in the first line of *Sea Haiku*. Why do you think the poet chose these two words?

c Think of two powerful adjectives of your own to describe the sea.

d Find an adverb in *Tanka* that describes how the boat moves. Can you think of another adverb that the poet could have used if the boat was moving in a different way?

## Writing

1. Decide whether you want to write a haiku, a tanka or a short rhyming poem.

2. Choose one of the pictures. Write some powerful words and phrases about how it makes you feel.

3. Write some other words to use.
   - If you are writing a rhyming poem, collect some rhyming words related to the picture.
   - If you are writing a haiku or tanka think carefully about the number of syllables in your words and how they fit together in a line.
   - See if you can think of a good simile and some alliterative words to use in your poem.

4. PAIR WORK. Write a first draft of your poem. Can you help each other to improve your poems?

## Reading and writing

> **Explanation texts**
> Explanation texts:
> - usually explain a process.
> - are written in the present simple tense.

**1** Read the explanation text below. Then answer the questions.

# Tsunami (soo-NAH-mee)

'Tsunami' is a Japanese word. 'Tsu' means harbour and 'nami' means wave.

### What is a tsunami?

A tsunami is a gigantic sea wave that can race across the ocean and cause a huge amount of damage when it reaches land.

### What causes a tsunami?

1. A tsunami is often caused by an earthquake on the sea bed. There is a sudden movement so the rocks start to move slowly. They crumble and break because they are near a fault line. This makes shock waves spread out.

2. When the shock waves reach the surface, they push the water up into a series of very long waves. At first these are only about half a metre high. They can travel as fast as some jet planes and they sweep rapidly across the ocean, towards the coastline.

3. At last the waves get closer to the land and the sea water gets shallower. This makes the first wave start to slow down, so the waves behind it catch up. The waves join up into a dangerous, towering wall of water which can be as high as 35 metres.

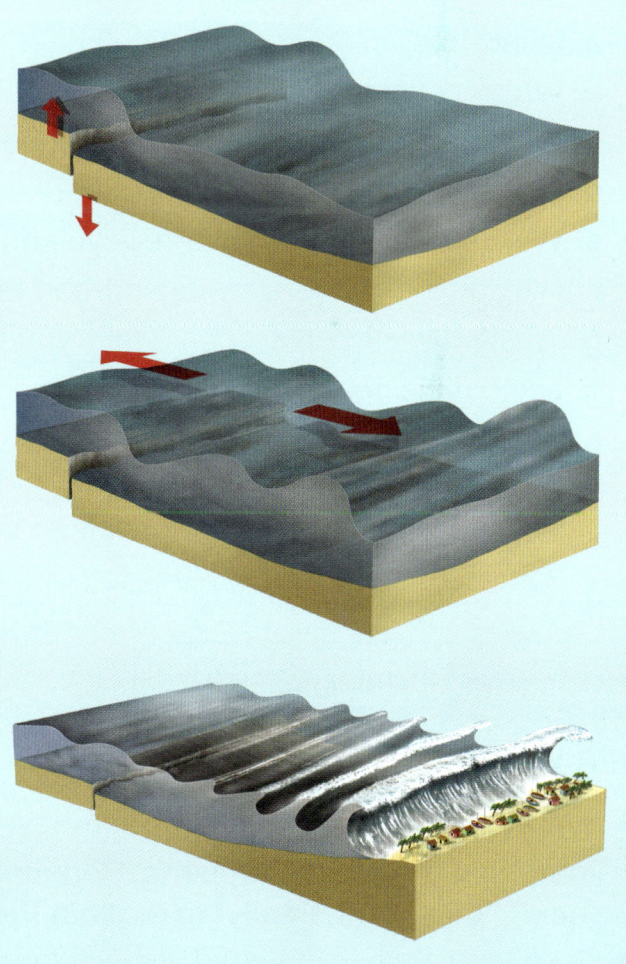

**4** Eventually, the wave crashes onto the land. It brings floods and damage to many places along the coast and sometimes far inland.

**2 Write the answers to the questions below.**

a Is this text fiction or non-fiction?
b Which country does the word 'tsunami' come from?
c What causes the sudden movement on the sea bed?
d At first, are the waves high or low?
e Which adverb in section 1 tells you how the rocks move?
f Why do the waves slow down when they get near the coast?
g Which adjective in section 3 tells you that the waves become very tall?
h Look at the photo in section 4. What kind of damage can a tsunami do?
i Think of a heading for each of the four sections. Your heading should sum up the main point of each section.
j Why do you think the writer decided to use diagrams as well as words to explain how a tsunami works?

## Listening and speaking

**PAIR WORK.**

**1** Take turns to use the explanation text on pages 31–32 to explain out loud how a tsunami happens. Remember to use connectives like 'at first', 'next', 'then' and 'finally' to explain the order in which things happen.

**2** Help each other to improve your explanations. Practise until you can explain a tsunami clearly to someone else.

## Using adjectives and adverbs

### Adjectives
You already know that adjectives describe nouns.

Some adjectives are stronger or give us more meaning than others. For example: 'delicious' and 'exquisite' are stronger than 'nice'.

**1** Sort these words into two lists – adjectives and adverbs.

> grey  happy  sadly  sparkling
> gently  dark  fabulous
> dangerously  shallow  big
> hungrily  quickly

**2** Find an adjective with a similar meaning in the box.

> exhausted  gigantic  ravenous

a  huge
b  tired
c  hungry

### Adverbs and adverbial phrases

**Adverbs** describe verbs, for example:
- walk <u>slowly</u>
  verb    adverb
- run <u>fast</u>
  verb    adverb
- whistle <u>happily</u>
  verb    adverb

Adverbs often – but not always – end in *–ly*.

The verb and the adverb together make an **adverbial phrase**.

**3** Write out the sentences below. Think of an adjective or adverb to fill each gap.

a  Marti plodded _____ along the road.
b  The _____ wave caused a lot of damage to the town.
c  We ate our dinner _____ because we were very hungry.
d  Kamla's _____ cat is called Kiki.
e  Our _____ boat was soon capsized by the _____ waves.
f  The rabbits ran _____ around the garden.

**4** Copy the sentences below. Underline the adverbial phrases.

a  Tsunamis sweep rapidly across the ocean.
b  My boat bobs gently on the waves.
c  The rain lashes roughly against the windows.

# Spelling

## Word families

Word families are groups of words with similar meanings, usually based on the same root word. For example:

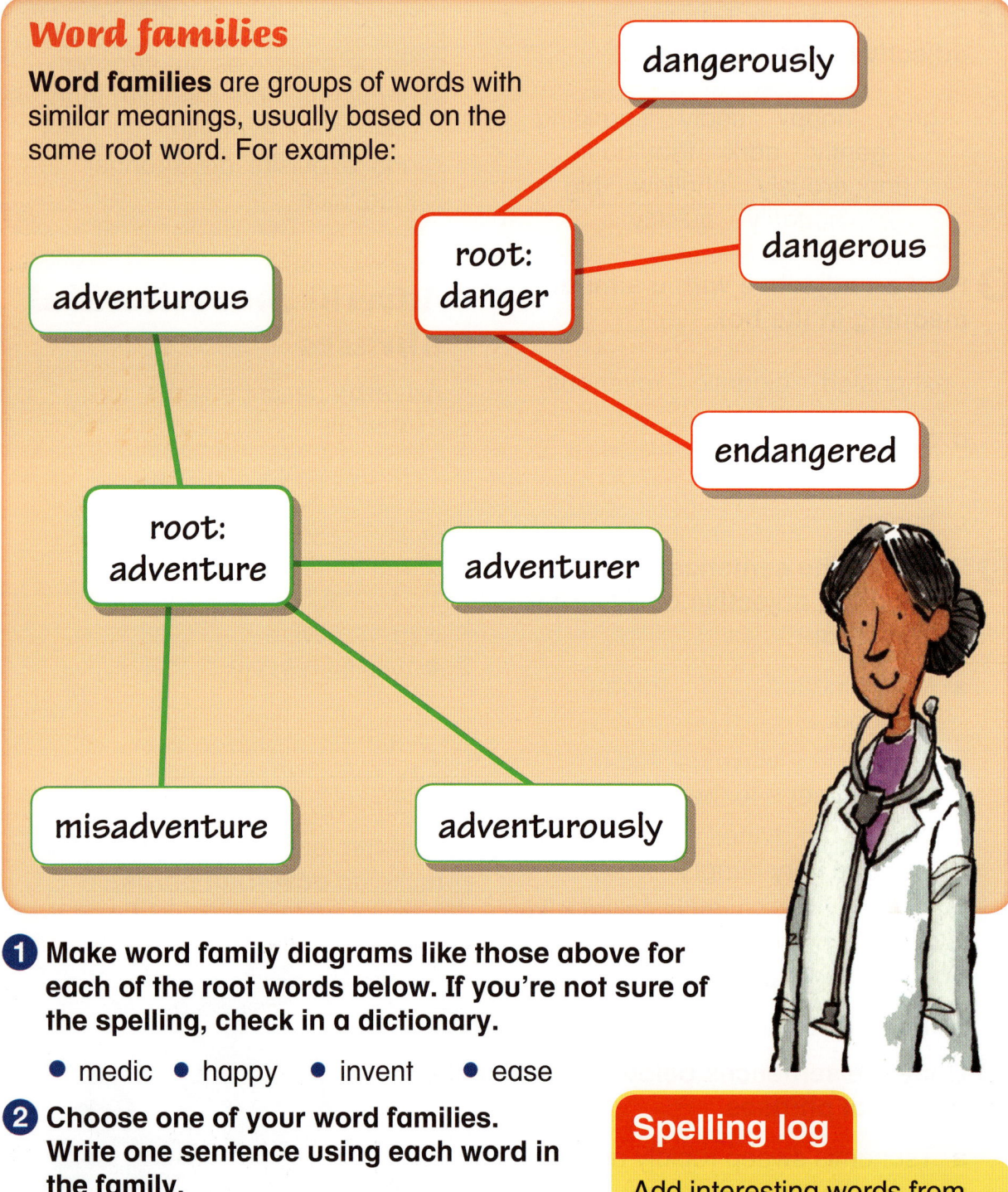

1. Make word family diagrams like those above for each of the root words below. If you're not sure of the spelling, check in a dictionary.

    - medic
    - happy
    - invent
    - ease

2. Choose one of your word families. Write one sentence using each word in the family.

**Spelling log**

Add interesting words from your word families to your spelling log.

## Reading, speaking and writing

**1** PAIR WORK. Look at the diagrams. Read the labels and captions. Use these to help you explain how sand is made.

# How sand is made

## 1 Rocks get broken down

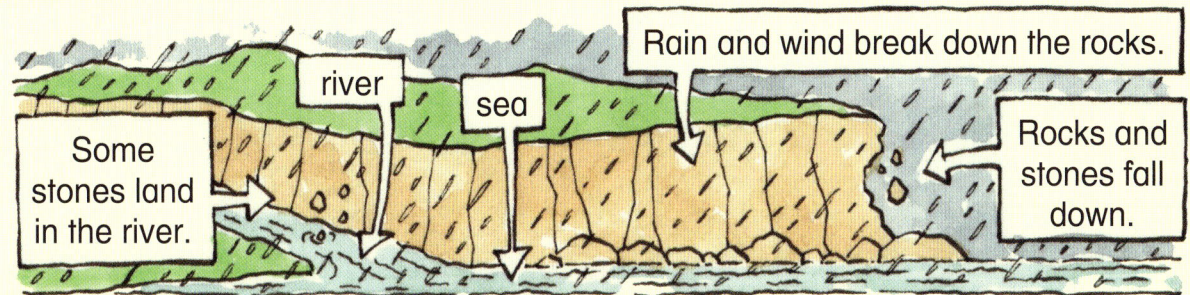

Rain and wind break down the rocks.

Some stones land in the river.

Rocks and stones fall down.

river

sea

## 2 Stones travel to the sea

Rocks and stones are carried by the river.

The river takes the stones to the sea.

river

## 3 The sea breaks down the stones

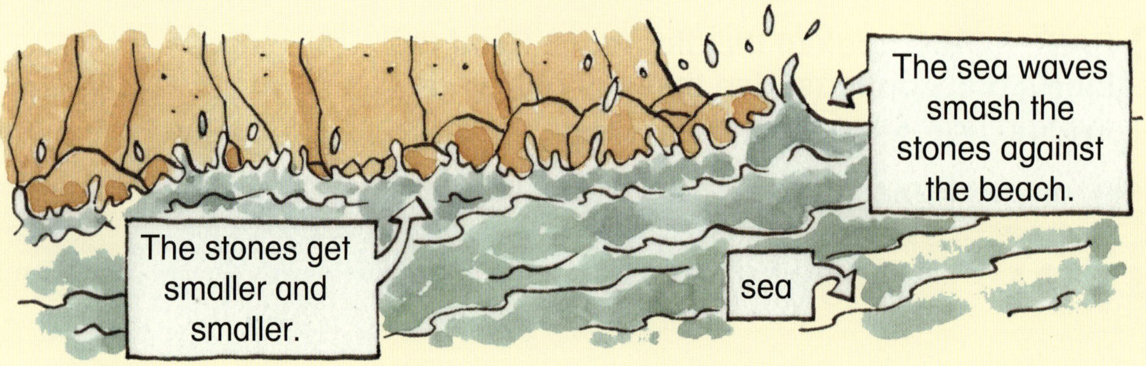

The sea waves smash the stones against the beach.

The stones get smaller and smaller.

sea

## 4 Sand is formed

The tiny pieces end up on the beach as sand.

The sea breaks the stones into tiny pieces.

**2** Practise explaining how sand is made. Then write an explanation text about it. Your text must have four paragraphs.

## Writing

Plan and write your own explanation text. Draw some diagrams to go with it.

### Step 1: Planning

**1** Decide what you would like to write your explanation about. Here are some ideas to help you – or you can choose another idea of your own.

- What causes rain?
- How are fossils made?
- Why is it dark at night?
- How does yeast make bread rise?
- What happens to your food when you eat it?

**2** Do some research to find out more about the idea you have chosen. Use books or the internet. Make notes and draw some diagrams to help you explain what happens.

**3** Use your notes to plan how you will write your explanation. Decide if you will do this on a computer or by hand.

**4** Use your plan to help you write your explanation text and draw the diagrams to go with it.

## Step 2: Redrafting and revising

**5** Show your text to someone else and ask them to comment on it.

**6** Consider the changes that the other person suggests. If you think they are good ones, add them to your explanation. Then read your work and edit it carefully.

**7** Write a final version of your text. Make the text and the diagrams look as good as you can.

### Remember!

When others are giving you feedback about your work, you should:

- listen carefully and politely to the comments.
- ask questions if you are not sure what the other person means.

### Thinking time

Talk about the feedback you received on your work.

How did it help you improve your text?

What feedback can you give to others that will help them?

# 4 Other people, other places

## Listening and speaking

**1** Listen as your teacher reads you a story from Eritrea called *The Clever Farmer*. You will hear the story twice.

**2** While you are listening for the second time think about the setting and the characters. Make some notes about:

- where the story is set.
- what the place is like.
- who the main characters are.
- what the characters are like.

**3** PAIR WORK. Talk about the setting and characters. Think of some words and phrases to describe the setting and characters. Choose your best ones to share with the rest of the class.

### Spelling log

Write any interesting words in your spelling log.

## Reading and writing

**1** Here is another African story. Read it once silently.

# Abunuwasi's House
### A story from Kenya

Abunuwasi was as cunning as a jackal, and smarter than a tree full of monkeys. Everyone knew it! He had the knack of getting his own way despite everything. If you don't believe me, just listen to this story …

Not so long ago, Abunuwasi built a house for himself. It had an upstairs and a downstairs. Abunuwasi decided to live downstairs, and he sold the upstairs to a merchant. The merchant was rich and greedy, and he knew he could live cheaply in Abunuwasi's house, so for a few years the two of them shared the house and both of them were happy.

However, one day, Abunuwasi decided he wanted to leave town and move somewhere far away. Perhaps he had annoyed too many people locally, or perhaps he just wanted a change of scene. Either way,

Abunuwasi hoped that the merchant who owned the top half of his house would agree to buy the bottom half. Then Abunuwasi could use the money to build a new house somewhere else.

Unfortunately for Abunuwasi, the greedy merchant refused. He was hoping that if he didn't buy Abunuwasi's part of the house, Abunuwasi would get fed up waiting, and just leave town anyway. That way, the merchant might end up getting the whole house for free.

But Abunuwasi was too cunning for that. He got together all his friends, and gave each of them a heavy mallet. Abunuwasi got his friends to stand all around the house with their mallets, and he went upstairs to talk to the merchant.

"Good day, my friend," said Abunuwasi to the merchant. "I've come to tell you that since I have been unable to sell my part of the house, I've hired some strong men to destroy it. You can see them out there, with their mallets. I thought I'd better let you know, so that you can do what you need to do to save your part of the house."

Well, of course, if Abunuwasi knocked down the bottom half of the house, there was no hope for the top half! So the greedy merchant hurriedly changed his mind and bought Abunuwasi's half of the house. And now Abunuwasi had the money he needed to start a new life ... a long, long way away!

**2** Talk about the questions below. Then write the answers.

a Where is the story set?
b Who lived downstairs in Abunuwasi's house?
c Why did Abunuwasi want to sell his part of the house to the merchant?
d Why didn't the merchant want to buy Abunuwasi's part of the house?
e Explain how Abunuwasi got the merchant to buy his part of the house.
f Why do you think Abunuwasi started his new life 'a long, long way away'?
g The writer describes Abunuwasi as 'as cunning as a jackal and smarter than a tree full of monkeys'. Do you think this is a good description? Why or why not?
h Write your own description of the merchant, beginning 'As greedy as ...'.
i Quantifiers are words like 'all', 'some' and 'neither', which tell us how many things or people we are talking about. Find and write three sentences from the story that use quantifiers. Then write your own sentences using these quantifiers.

### Thinking deeper

- Can you think of reasons why stories are so valuable? Why was telling stories an important role in the past?
- How does this writer capture the idea of telling stories out loud? What would it be like listening to this story around a camp fire?
- Change the opening sentence of this story and act out telling this story to your partner. Make sure it is engaging, dramatic and exciting for them.

## Punctuation, speaking and reading

### Direct speech

Stories often include the words the characters *say* to each other. This is called **direct speech**.

The words people speak are written inside speech marks: " ".

**1** PAIR WORK. Read the sentences below. Decide which words are direct speech.

- You've broken my best pen said Abbie crossly
- No I haven't said Li. It was broken when I found it
- Never mind, Abbie. You can borrow my pen said Nadine

Abunuwasi's first bit of speech is "Good day, my friend."

At the end of the sentence we need to add 'said Abunuwasi to the merchant', so we don't put a full stop after 'friend' — we use a comma before the speech marks instead.

Now look at Abunuwasi's second bit of speech:

"I've come to tell you that since I have been unable to sell my part of the house, I've hired some strong men to destroy it."

It ends in a full stop before the speech marks, because we don't have to add anything extra at the end of this sentence.

**2** Write the sentences from question 1. Add all the missing punctuation.

**3** PAIR WORK. Reread *Abunuwasi's House.* Imagine what the merchant said to Abunuwasi when he realised he had to buy Abunuwasi's part of the house after all. Act out this conversation.

# Reading and writing

## Story structure

Good stories often have five stages.
- They start with an **introduction** that sets up the story and introduces the main character and setting.
- Then there is a **problem** or **build-up** – something starts to happen.
- The problem reaches a **climax** (often with **conflict** between the characters). This is often the most exciting part of the story.
- There is a **resolution** – where the problem is solved.
- The story ends with a **conclusion** that ties up the loose ends and leaves the reader feeling satisfied.

**PAIR WORK.** Read *Abunuwasi's House* again. Work out how the story fits into the five story stages. Then write a summary of what happens at each stage of the story.

**Use the headings below.**

Introduction    Problem/Build-up    Climax/Conflict    Resolution    Conclusion

# Punctuation

Write out the sentences below. Add apostrophes where they are needed.

a  Annas eyes are blue and Ellas are brown.
b  The girls shoes are under their beds.
c  Dad forgot to make the childrens sandwiches.
d  Its Michaels birthday, but he isnt very happy.
e  I havent seen Marias sister today.

## Apostrophes

We use apostrophes to show:
- where there are missing letters ('don't', 'can't', 'wouldn't')
- possession – when something belongs to someone ('Ahmed's cat'; 'the family's car'; 'the men's boots'; 'the goats' food').

We don't use apostrophes for plurals ('apostrophes', not 'apostrophe's').

## Reading and writing

**1** This is a Native American story. Read it to yourself silently.

# The Brave Baby
### retold by Malachy Doyle

The chief was brave and fierce, so many people were afraid of him. But a wise old woman said, "I know someone who is not afraid of you."

The chief was surprised. "Who is this man?" he cried. "Show him to me!"

The old woman took him to her tent.

"Where is this man?" said the chief.
"I cannot see him."

"It is not a man," said the old woman. "It is Wasso, the baby girl." Wasso sat on a blanket, playing with a stick.

"Why is this baby not afraid of me?" said the chief. "Everyone is afraid of me! Come here, child!" he cried. But Wasso only smiled at him.

"Come here, I said!" The chief was angry with the little girl. Wasso stopped smiling and looked up at the chief.

"You must do as I say, child!" cried the chief.

Wasso looked at the man who was shouting at her, and she began to cry. Wasso cried and she cried, but she still would not go to the chief. So the chief began to dance. It was a special dance – a dance to make people do as he said.

44

Wasso stopped crying. She liked the dance. She looked up at the chief and she smiled.

The chief did another dance, to make her come to him. But Wasso only laughed.

The chief danced some more, but still the baby would not do as he said. Still she would not go to him. The chief danced and danced. Wasso smiled and laughed ... and then she fell asleep.

"You see," said the old woman to the chief. "Here is someone who is not afraid of you."

"You are right," said the chief. "Wasso is braver than me. She is a very brave baby."

The chief was too tired to be angry any more. He liked the brave baby. He lay down in the tent and fell fast asleep.

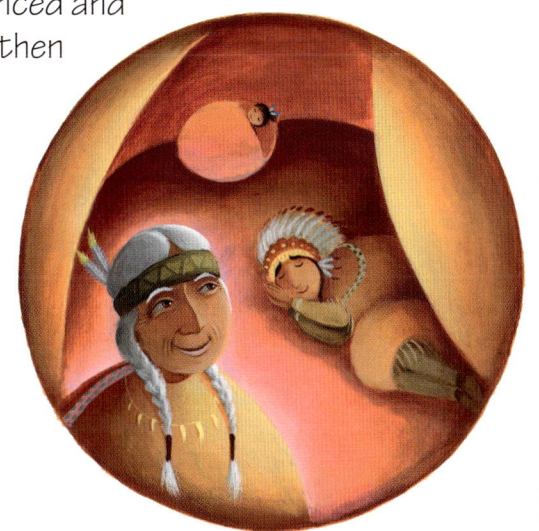

**2** **Write the answers to the questions below.**

a What was it about the chief's character that made people feel afraid?
b Why did the chief expect to see a man in the tent?
c How did Wasso behave when she first saw the chief?
d When did Wasso start to cry?
e What did the chief do to make Wasso go to him?
f How did the chief feel at the end of the story?
g Which two adjectives in the box below could be used to describe the chief? Use these two adjectives in a sentence about the chief.

> proud  ancient  courageous  weak  dishonest  ignorant  sad  helpful

h Think of an adjective to describe the wise old woman. Use this adjective in a sentence about her.
i Use the headings 'Introduction', 'Problem/Build-up', 'Climax/Conflict', 'Resolution' and 'Conclusion' and write notes to show which part of this story belongs under each heading.

## Speaking, listening and writing

**GROUP WORK.**

1. Reread *The Brave Baby.* The story does not include much detail.

2. Act out the story together.

3. Now go through the sections of the story and think what you could add to make each section more detailed. For example:

   - **Introduction:** Can you add more details about the characters and setting?
   - **Problem/Build-up:** Can you add more information about how the chief feels and more conversation between the chief and the wise woman?
   - **Climax/Conflict:** Can you make the chief's dancing sound funnier? Can you add more about how Wasso reacts to the chief?
   - **Resolution:** Can you add more details or more explanation about why the chief has changed his mind about Wasso?
   - **Conclusion:** What do you think the chief learnt in this story? What is the story trying to tell us? Can you add a few more sentences to explain this?

4. Make notes to help you remember what you are going to add to the story.

5. Write a new version of the story including your extra bits. You can change the beginning or the end of the story.

## Writing

**1** **Look at the following simple sentence.** *The chief was angry with the little girl.* **Rewrite the sentence using more expressive and descriptive language.**

- Add an extra adjective to describe the chief.
- Use a stronger adjective instead of 'angry'.
- Use a simile to describe how angry the chief was.
- Replace 'little girl' with a more interesting description of Wasso.

The _____ chief was _____ with the _____ girl.

**2** **Rewrite the last three sentences of the story. Make the language more expressive and descriptive. Use adverbs or adverbial phrases to give extra information about the verbs. Make the sentences as interesting as possible.**

### Thinking deeper

Imagine you were the chief for a day. How would you stand, talk and walk? Now act out that person.

Write ten words about how being that person made you feel. How do you think you looked to others?

## Spelling

### Words with more than one syllable

There are some tricks you can try to help you spell longer words.
- Look at the word to see if it has any common prefixes (like *un–*, *dis–*, *super–*, *some–*) or suffixes (like *–ed*, *–er*, *–ing*).
- If it does, what is the **root word**?
- Spotting the root word can help you spell the whole word. Look for any spelling patterns that you already know.
- If there isn't a prefix or suffix, split the word up into syllables. Say the word and work out which syllable in the word is stressed the most. Looking at each syllable can help you to say and spell the word.

1. Try the ideas on pages 47 and 65 to help you remember how to spell the two-syllable words below from *The Brave Baby*.

   a someone
   b surprised
   c blanket
   d angry
   e afraid
   f cannot
   g playing
   h shouting

> **Spelling log**
>
> Add any tricky or interesting words with more than one syllable to your spelling log.

2. Write your own sentences using each of the words above. Remember to spell them correctly.

## Using verb tenses

**PAIR WORK.**

1. Look at the sentences in *The Brave Baby* and decide what tense the story is in.

2. Write a new ending for the story. Explain what happens after Wasso and the chief wake up.

   - Write at least four sentences. Include some direct speech.
   - Use the past tense for the sentences without speech and the present or future tense for the sentences with speech.

### Past, present and future

Every sentence needs a verb! Verbs can be in the past, present or future tense. Normally writers use the past tense when they are telling a story – for example, 'The chief <u>was</u> brave and fierce, so many people <u>were</u> afraid of him.'

But the direct speech in a story is often in the present tense, like this: "Wasso <u>is</u> braver than me. She <u>is</u> a very brave baby." Sometimes, direct speech uses the future tense, for example, "I <u>will</u> never give up!"

## Writing

Write your own story. Follow the five stages as you plan your story. You can use a story you already know as an idea or make up a new story of your own.

Your story should follow the five-stage structure:

Introduction → Problem/Build-up → Climax/Conflict → Resolution → Conclusion

### Step 1: Planning

- Decide what kind of story you want to write. Make some notes to remind you.
- Who is your main character? Write a character profile describing them.
- Plan your story using the five-stage structure.
- If you are using an old story, think about how you want your version to be different.
- Write some notes to remind you what needs to happen at each stage of the story.
- If you are writing a new story, think about how you are going to interest the reader.

- Use your plan to write your story.
- Each section needs to be at least one or two paragraphs long.
- Remember to include some direct speech.

### Remember!

You can change the beginning or ending of a story to make your own version. You can also change the characters or the setting.

## Step 2: Redrafting and revising

Read your first draft out loud to yourself and make corrections.

Let your partner read your story and make suggestions to improve the story.

Write a final version of your story, including any changes that you think improve it. You could also add some pictures if you like.

### Thinking time

Which story did you enjoy most? What have you learned about other cultures from the stories in this unit?

# 5 The only problem is …

**Reading, listening and speaking**

PAIR WORK.

**1** Take turns to read the poem below out loud.

## The Youngest

I'm the youngest in our house
so it goes like this:

My brother comes in and says:
"Tell him to clear the fluff
out from under his bed."
Mum says,
"Clear the fluff
out from under your bed."
Father says,
"You heard what your mother said."
"What?" I say.
"The fluff," he says.
"Clear the fluff
out from under your bed."
So I say,
"There's fluff under his bed too,
you know."
So father says,
"But we're talking about the fluff
under your bed."
"You will clear it up
won't you?" Mum says.

So now my brother – all puffed up –
says,
"Clear the fluff
out from under your bed,
clear the fluff
out from under your bed."
Now I'm angry. I am angry.
So I say – what shall I say?
I say,
"Shuttup stinks
YOU CAN'T RULE MY LIFE."

by Michael Rosen

**2** Talk about the questions below.

- Do you feel sorry for anyone in this poem? Who and why?
- Do you think it was fair that everyone kept asking the narrator to clear the fluff out from under his bed?
- Do you think the poem is funny? If so, which parts are funniest?
- Do you think the poem is realistic?
- Why do you think the narrator is so cross at the end of the poem? Would you be cross?
- What else could the narrator have said at the end of the poem? With your partner, think of a new ending.
- Has anything like this ever happened in your family? Take turns to tell your partner about it.
- Choose one of your stories to tell the whole class.

**3** Team up with another pair. Decide who is going to play each part (the narrator, mother, father and brother). Practise reading the poem out loud as a group.

## Reading

**1** Before you read the story below read the title and look carefully at the picture. Who are the characters? What do you think this story is about?

**2** Read the story silently to yourself.

# Meeting Mr Faulkner

*Jude and Kitty are meeting Gerald Faulkner for the first time.*

He stepped inside. He was Mum's height, a little tubby, and he had silvery hair. His suit was nowhere near as smart as any of Simon's. There again, he wasn't a posh banker, though he did have the most enormous box of chocolates tucked under one arm.

He shifted the chocolates, and shook hands.

"Judith," he said. "Right?"

She nodded. I sidled out of the shadow.

"And Kitty."

He smiled, and kept his hand stuck out for a moment, but I pretended that I hadn't noticed it. And after one of those infinitesimal little pauses of his, he handed the huge box of chocolates to Jude.

They were those rich, dark, expensive, chocolate-coated cream mints. I've had a passion for them all my life. The box was three layers deep at the very least. I saw Jude's eyes widen to saucers.

"Are these for Mum?" she asked.

"No. They're for you."

He could have meant either you, or you two. It wasn't clear. As he spoke, he was looking at Jude, but he did glance at me briefly. It was terribly clever. It meant that when I didn't pile straight in with Jude, thanking him lavishly, he wasn't in the slightest embarrassed. He didn't have to be, you see. He might not have meant to include me at all.

"I'll tell Mum."

Jude rushed upstairs, clutching her booty to her chest, and Gerald Faulkner and I were left alone in the hall. I thought I'd discomfit him with my silence, but no, not at all. He simply swivelled away as though he wanted to inspect the pictures on the wall, and peered closely at a photo of me as a toddler.

"What a face!" he said admiringly. (I wasn't quite sure what he meant by that.) "It looks as if it might be you."

Really cunning, right? He doesn't actually ask if it's me, and then he can't look silly if I don't answer.

Just then Floss padded in through the front door, and started rubbing up against his trouser legs as if she'd known and loved him all her life. He stopped to pet her. "Puss, puss, puss." I thought now he'd be bound to try and get me to speak. It's hard to fondle someone else's cat in front of them, and not ask its name. But Gerald Faulkner's made of sterner stuff than that.

"Up you come, Buster," he said, scooping Floss up in his arms. "Who's a nice kitty?"

I wasn't quite sure what he meant by that, either. I was still trying to work it out (and Floss was still purring shamelessly) when Jude came thundering downstairs.

"Mum says to help yourself to a drink, and she'll be down in a minute."

"Right-ho."

He tipped the enraptured Floss into Jude's arms, and ambled past me with a nod. I wondered if he had been in our house before. How else would he know which door led into the kitchen?

from *Goggle-Eyes* by Anne Fine

**3** **Write the answers to the questions below.**

a Whose viewpoint is the story told from?
b Write out a sentence from the text that tells us Jude is very pleased with the chocolates.
c Why do you think Kitty doesn't speak to Gerald?
d What does Gerald do when Kitty does not talk to him?
e How would you have felt if you had been Gerald?
f Write out a sentence from the text that tells us that the cat likes Gerald.
g Why does Gerald call the cat Buster?
h 'He tipped the **enraptured** Floss into Jude's arms, and **ambled** past me with a nod.' Rewrite this sentence using different words that mean the same as 'enraptured' and 'ambled'. Use your dictionary if you need to.
i Find three sentences that use powerful verbs. Write the sentences out and underline the verbs.
j From just this text what do you think Kitty is like?
Write a paragraph to describe her.
k Why does Kitty think Gerald has been to their house before?
l Do you think Kitty will make friends with Gerald in the end? Say why you think this.

## Using adverbs

### Adverbs and adverbial phrases

Adverbs are used to add more detail to verbs. For example, in the phrase 'thanking him lavishly', 'lavishly' is an adverb that means 'very much' or 'in an exaggerated way'. It goes with the verb 'thanking' – it tells us how Kitty might have thanked Gerald.

Look at the words 'Jude rushed upstairs, clutching her booty to her chest'. Here, the phrase 'clutching her booty to her chest' tells us more about how Jude rushed upstairs. It is an adverbial phrase, because it is a whole group of words that does the same job as an adverb. It adds more detail to the verb 'rushed'.

**1** Write out the sentences below. Underline the adverbs or adverbial phrases and draw a ring round the verbs that go with them.

   a  He did glance at me briefly.
   b  He swivelled away as though he wanted to inspect the pictures on the walls.
   c  He peered closely at a photo of me as a toddler.
   d  "What a face!" he said admiringly.

**2** Rewrite the sentences below. Change the adverbs so that they are more interesting.

   a  "I forgot my packed lunch," said Samir sadly.
   b  Mara walked away quickly.

**3** Rewrite the sentences below. Add adverbial phrases to give more detail about the verbs.

   a  I ran down the road.
   b  Dean started laughing.

# Subject-verb agreement

## Subject-verb agreement

All sentences need a **subject** and a **verb**. In the sentence 'She nodded', the subject is 'she' and the verb is 'nodded'.

The subject and verb in a sentence have to **agree**. This means using the correct form of the verb to go with the subject. A plural subject needs a plural verb, and a singular subject needs a singular verb. For example:

- Plural: The cats **are** miaowing.
- Singular: The cat **is** miaowing.

Some subjects also have an **object**. For example, in the sentence 'She nodded her head', the subject is 'she', the verb is 'nodded' and the object is 'her head'.

**1** Rewrite the sentences below. Change the verb so that it agrees with the subject.

a My hamster are eating.
b The children is playing.
c I are tired.

**2** Write out the statements below. Draw a straight line under the subject, a wiggly line under the verb and a circle round the object, like this:
We saw the (Eiffel Tower)

a I ate the cake.
b The boys were wearing sports clothing.
c Miss Beckson was angry with Class 2.

## Reading and writing

**1** Read the poem below.

# Eleven Years Old

I'm old enough
to work in the fields,
my grandmother says:
your limbs are young
and strong,
your mind won't rust,
we need the extra hands
to tend the crop
and feed the goats
and till this ungrateful land.

Maybe
I'll go to school
when the crop is in,
when we take the few yams
from the soil,
then I'll wear a new dress,
and leave when it's early day,
for it's only one mile to the school.

by Dionne Brand

**Poems**

Poems can have:
- interesting or unusual words.
- lines that are repeated.
- figurative language such as similes.
- rhyme and rhythm.

**2** Write the answers to the questions below.

  a  What crops and animals are kept on the farm in this poem?
  b  Why does the narrator of the poem have to work on the farm?
  c  How do you think the narrator feels about working on the farm? What would she rather be doing?
  d  What does 'your mind won't rust' mean?
  e  How is the narrator's life similar to yours? How is it different?
  f  Write down two or more things which are similar about the poems *The Youngest* and *Eleven Years Old*.
  g  Write down two or more things which are different in the two poems.

## Listening and speaking

**PAIR WORK.**

**1** Reread *The Youngest* and *Eleven Years Old* aloud.

  - Make your reading as expressive as you can.
  - Think about the meaning of the words as you say them. Look at the punctuation for clues about how to say each line.

**2** Decide which of the two poems you prefer. Talk about your reasons. Make notes to remind you why you chose this poem.

**3** Practise reading and performing the poem you chose. Read it through several times until it sounds really good.

**4** Perform the poem to the rest of the class. Start by explaining why you like the poem and why you chose it. Use the notes you made earlier to help with this.

# Writing

Plan and write your own poem about a problem you or someone else has had.

## Step 1: Planning

**1** Talk about ideas for your poem with your partner or group. You could write about a time when:
- you were scared.
- something sad happened.
- something went wrong at school or home.
- you were worried about something.

You don't have to write about your own life if you don't want to – you could borrow an idea from a story or a film you have seen.

**2** Practise telling your partner about your idea as if you were telling a story. Try to make it sound as exciting as possible – like Michael Rosen and Dionne Brand do in their poems.

**3** Look at the poems on pages 27, 51 and 57 and decide what type of poem you want to write. Then make some notes to help you write your idea as a poem.

**4** Use your notes to help you write a draft of your poem.

## Step 2: Redrafting and revising

**5** Read your first draft out loud to yourself and make corrections.

**6** Now read the poem out loud to your partner. Can they make any suggestions to improve it?

**7** Decide if you want to write the poem by hand or on the computer. Think about the punctuation that you want to include.

## Reading

Read the story below.

### The New Boy

*Amrik has just arrived from India and speaks no English. Fortunately, at his new school, there is a girl called Kamla who can talk to him in Hindi and help him learn English.*

Kamla and Kate took Amrik over to their table. He sat down rather awkwardly. At his village school in India all the children used to sit cross-legged on the ground under the mango tree.

Kamla pointed to each child on her table and introduced them.

"This is Kate, Justin, Nigel and Rachel," she said. Then she prodded the table and said, "and this is our table!"

Amrik looked solemnly at each child. "Kate, Jus ... teen, Ni ... gel, Rachel ..." then he prodded the table and said, "Our table!" Everyone laughed and clapped.

At playtime Kamla and Kate took Amrik out into the playground. He stood in a corner with his back to the wall looking very frightened. Ever since he arrived in England he had felt puzzled. He could see no brown earth under his feet – just concrete. Wherever you walked, the ground was hard. No wonder his father had made him wear shoes and socks. He could hardly see the sky. It seemed lost up there between tall blocks of buildings, and the sky was the colour of concrete – grey! In India you did not have to look for the earth and sky, it was all around you. And you could not lose the sun as they seemed to here.

"Kamla, where is the earth? Where are the wheatfields? Where do they grow rice and mustard seed? Where are the fruit trees? The mango and guava groves? Can oxen plough this hard ground? How do you eat?"

"We live in a city, Amrik," explained Kamla. "The food is grown in the countryside. We buy our wheat and rice and fruit from the shops."

"Where are the water wells?" asked Amrik looking around. "I'm thirsty. Are the wells also under all this hard stone?" He looked in despair around the playground.

from *Kamla and Kate* by Jamila Gavin

## Comprehension

**GROUP WORK. Talk about the questions below. Then write the answers.**

a  What language does Amrik speak?
b  Why does Amrik sit down 'rather awkwardly' at the table?
c  Why is Amrik puzzled and frightened?
d  Write down three differences between England (where Amrik lives now) and the part of India where Amrik used to live.
e  Why did everyone laugh and clap when Amrik spoke?
f  How does Kamala help Amrik on his first day?
g  The writer of this story, Jamila Gavin, moved from India to Britain as a child herself. How do you think this might have influenced her writing?

## Reading and writing

1. Reread *The New Boy*. There are eight paragraphs. Write down the reason why the writer started a new paragraph each time.

2. Write a new paragraph to go at the end of the story.

### Paragraphs

In stories, there are two main reasons for starting a new paragraph:

- something new happens in the story
- a new speaker says something.

## Spelling

1. PAIR WORK. Reread *The New Boy*. Find all the words that contain the letter string *ou*.

2. Now write the words in lists. Group them so that words which are said the same are together.

Sometimes the same letter string can be said in more than one way. For example, there are lots of ways of saying the letter string *ou*.

3. Look at books, posters and leaflets and see how many other *ou* words you can add to your lists.

## Words with *ough*

The letter string *ough* can be pronounced in a lot of different ways.

1. There is one word with the letter string *ough* in *The New Boy*. Can you find it?
2. Read these *ough* words out loud. Then write them out, grouping together the words where *ough* has the same sound:

   cough   bought   ought   rough
   thought   borough   bough   through
   dough   drought   enough   thorough

3. How many more *ough* words can you find? Add them to the lists.

# Writing

### Step 1: Planning

1. Imagine you are like Amrik in *The New Boy* – you have just moved to a new country and a new school and you don't speak the same language as everyone else. Think about these things and make some notes.
   - How would you feel?
   - How would you want people to treat you?
   - What might go well?
   - What might be very difficult for you?

2. Write about how you might feel and what might happen. You need to write at least four paragraphs. Make a paragraph plan, with a heading and a description for each paragraph.

### Step 2: Redrafting and revising

3. Read your draft out loud to yourself or to your partner.

4. Write a final version, making any changes that you need to make. Remember to use your best handwriting.

## Thinking time

How do you feel when you have to deal with issues? Did you identify with the issues in the poems or stories in this unit?

# 6 Making the headlines

## Reading, listening and speaking

> **Newspaper reports**
> Newspaper reports usually include:
> - a headline.
> - a summary sentence.
> - quotations from people involved in the story.
> - photographs.

**1** Skim the newspaper article below to get a quick idea of what it is about. Look at the headline, bold text, photo and caption.

# Malala's award

**MALALA Yousafzai from Pakistan has become the youngest person ever to win the Nobel Peace Prize.**

The 17 year old learned she had won the award in a Chemistry lesson, when another teacher came into the classroom to tell her.

Malala has been recognised for her hard work promoting the right for all children, especially girls, to go to school. Around 57 million children worldwide don't get that chance.

When Malala was 15, she was shot on her way to school, for speaking out about the subject of girls' education. Malala was badly hurt in the attack but was flown to Britain for treatment and has recovered well. She lives in Britain now, and continues her campaigning.

Malala said: "When I found I had won the Nobel Peace Prize I decided I would not leave my school, I would finish my school time. I went to the Physics lessons, I learnt. I went to the English lesson. I considered it like a normal day … I'm proud I'm the first Pakistani and the first young woman or the first young person who is getting this award. It's a great honour for me."

The Nobel Peace Prize is one of a number of Nobel prizes given to people or organisations who have made outstanding achievements in different areas. It is one of the most respected awards in the world. Malala shares the award with Kailash Satyarthi, from India, who has worked for children's rights and against child slavery.

*Malala attending the Woman of the Year awards in 2013*

**2** **PAIR WORK. Talk about the article. Talk about the questions below.**

- What impression do you get of Malala? Describe her to your partner.
- Why do you think Malala says the prize is 'a great honour for me'?

**3** **Write the answers to the questions below about *Malala's award*.**

a Reread the article and answer the **who**, **what**, **when**, **where** and **why** questions (see the box above).

b Why do you think the first sentence of the article is in bold type?

c How many children around the world are not able to go to school, according to the article?

d How did Malala react when she heard she had won the Nobel Peace Prize?

e Name one thing that is unusual about Malala as a Nobel Peace Prize winner.

f Reread the last paragraph of the article. Write one sentence to sum up the main point of the paragraph.

g Headlines normally sum up the message of the article in just a few words. Write a new headline for this article. Use five words or fewer.

---

**Newspaper articles**

**Who, what, when, where ... and why**

Newspaper articles usually answer these questions:

- **Who** is the article about?
- **What** have they done, or what happened to them?
- **When** did it happen?
- **Where** did it happen?
- **Why** or how did it happen?

Journalists often give the answers to these questions right at the start of the article, so that the reader can quickly see what the article is about.

---

**Thinking deeper**

Malala is a hero to many people. In your groups, take turns to give your ideas about heroes. Write or draw pictures on the sheet of paper your teacher gives you. Then read what others have written.

Here are some questions to think about:

- Who is your hero and why?
- Do you have the same values and beliefs as your hero? Give an example.
- Could you be a hero to someone else? How?

## Spelling

1. Write a list of ten words from the article *Malala's award* that have more than two syllables.

2. Practise spelling the words until you can remember them without looking.

3. Write some sentences of your own using each of the words.

4. Read the Spelling help box. Which way do you think would work best for you?

### Spelling log

Add these words to your spelling log and try to use them in your own writing.

Words with several syllables can be tricky to spell. But if you break long words down into their separate parts, it is easier to remember how they are spelled. Look at page 47 for some more ideas.

### Spelling help!

- Say a word exactly as it is spelled. This helps with words that have silent letters, like 'knife' and 'lamb' (say 'kenife' and 'lam**b**') – and with words where we don't say every sound, like 'parliament', 'television' and 'February' (say 'par-lee-a-ment' and 'te-le-vis-i-on' and 'Feb-roo-air-ee').

- Make up a 'mnemonic' – a funny phrase that helps you remember the spelling. For example, to learn how to spell 'because', say to yourself, '**b**ig **e**lephants **c**an **a**lways **u**nderstand **s**mall **e**lephants'.

## Punctuation

Commas are often used to separate out a part of a sentence that:
- gives the reader extra information
- isn't essential in order to understand the rest of the sentence.

For example:

'Malala has been recognised for her hard work promoting the right for all children, especially girls, to go to school.'

There are commas around the phrase 'especially girls' because it gives us a *little bit of extra information*.

If you took that phrase out of the sentence, the sentence would *still make sense without it*.

**1** Find and write one other sentence from the article that uses commas to give extra information or separate out information which isn't essential.

**Remember!**
Take the words inside the commas out of the sentence and see if it still makes sense.

**2** Write out the sentences below. Add the missing commas around the phrases that give extra information.

a Mei's cat called Fluffy was extremely fierce.
b My favourite food is pancakes especially with chocolate.
c Kamal's little sister at the age of only three won a singing competition.
d Our next-door neighbour Mr Fanelli grows delicious strawberries.
e I washed the dishes lots of them because I wanted to surprise my mother.

## Reading, speaking and writing

**1** Skim the article below. What do you think it is about? Then read it and answer the questions.

# Mini Mars mission

Talk about dreaming out of this world!

13-year-old American teenager Alyssa Carson plans to be the first person to set foot on Mars, and NASA seems to be backing her all the way.

The 'future Mars walker', as she refers to herself on her official Twitter page, is currently training to be an astronaut. She began training when she was only three years old! She already has her own codename – Blueberry.

She is already learning several languages and attending some tough Science classes as part of her training.

Alyssa exclusively told *First News*: "I want to go to Mars because I have so many questions that I want answered. For example, is there life? I am very determined. I have made it this far and I don't think I'll be changing my mind."

Watch this 'space' – we have high hopes for this big dreamer!

The first planned mission to Mars will be in 2033.

**2** **PAIR WORK.** Use the questions below to talk about the article on page 67. Then write your answers to the questions.

a What is the article mostly about? See if you can sum it up in just one sentence.

b What impression do you get of Alyssa from the article? Draw a spider diagram like the one below.

*Alyssa*

c Write a word or phrase describing Alyssa at the end of each line. You can add as many lines as you like.

d How do you feel about Alyssa's ambition? Would you want to do this yourself? Why, or why not?

e The journalist who wrote the article has included several puns – little jokes that are based on words to do with space. Write down as many as you can find.

f Why do you think the journalist used these puns?

g Do you think the first line of the article is effective in getting the reader's attention? Why, or why not?

h Find and write down at least one sentence that includes a fact and at least one sentence that includes an opinion.

i If Alyssa was 13 in 2014, when this article was published, how old is she likely to be by the time she leaves to go to Mars?

A pun is a play on different meanings of sounds of the same word. For example:
*Seven days without food makes one weak.*

## Writing

Plan and write your own newspaper article about something that has happened to an interesting person. The person can be someone you know in real life who has done something unusual and special or it can be someone famous like a sporting personality, musician, scientist or film star.

### Step 1: Planning

**1** Decide who you want to write about and what events you will report on. For example, you might choose:
- an adult you know who has done something interesting.
- someone who achieved a lot while they were still young.
- a child you know who has big ambitions for their life.
- a famous sportsperson, musician or scientist.
- someone else you find interesting.

> **Remember!**
> Think about the layout of your article. You can use different sizes of print for different parts. You can also use columns.

**2** Think about how you will research your article.
- If it is about someone you know, see if you can interview them about the events you want to write about. Remember to write down some of what they say as a quote — you can use the quote in your article.
- If it is about a famous person, look for newspaper and magazine articles about them. You may also be able to find out more about them on the internet. Look for interesting facts about them and try to find some good quotes, too.

**3** Make careful notes from your research.

**4** Write a first draft of your article.

## Step 2: Redrafting and revising

5. Read your first draft out loud to yourself or to a partner. Also check that all your sentences make sense and that you have used correct spellings and punctuation.

6. Write a final version of your article, including any corrections needed. Add a photo or a drawing of the person you wrote about, if you can.

**Remember!**

If you are using a computer, you can use the spellcheck, but read everything carefully too.

## Reading and writing

**Magazine articles**
Like newspaper articles, magazine articles also try to attract readers, but they are usually about events of general interest. They are not about daily events.

**1** Here are two pieces of writing from a children's magazine. Skim them first. Read the headings and look at the pictures to get an idea of what they are about.

# Fossil Hunt

Collecting fossils is a great hobby. Here's what you need to know if you want to be a fossil hunter!

## Where should you look?
It's easiest to find fossils in sedimentary rocks, such as mudstone and limestone. Fossils form when an animal or plant gets buried in mud or sand. Over a long, long time the grains of mud or sand turn into sedimentary rock, with the fossils inside.

You can look for fossils anywhere where there is sedimentary rock – beaches are often a good place. However, fields and farmland can be good too. If you are very lucky and live in the right place, you might even find a fossil in your garden!

## What kit do you need?
The best bit of kit is your eyes! If you go for a walk along a beach, you may spot fossils just lying among the shells and pebbles. Experienced grown-up fossil hunters sometimes use a hammer and chisel to get fossils out of the rocks, but that can be dangerous – and you don't need expensive tools to spot fossils.

## Staying safe
Sometimes good fossil-hunting places can be dangerous, because there might be a rock fall, or if you are by the sea, you could get cut off by the tide. That's why you should always go fossil-hunting with an adult.

## Starting your collection
When you find a fossil, make a label for it. The label should say:
- where and when you found the fossil.
- what type of rock you think you found it in.
- what type of fossil you think it is.

There are lots of good books and internet sites that will help you identify the fossils you find.

### Have fun!

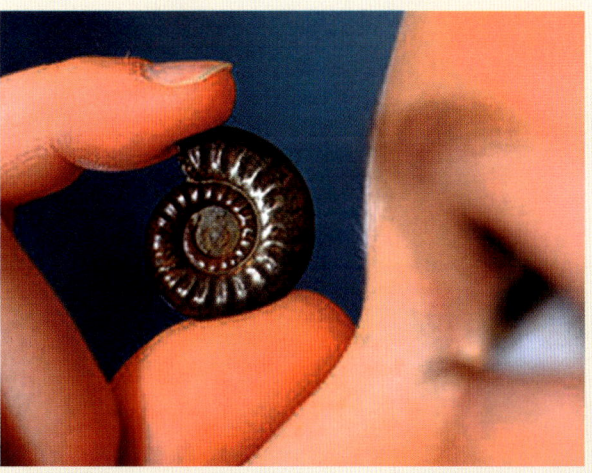

# Make your own fossil!

No luck finding real fossils? Don't despair! You can make your own (fake) fossils to amaze your friends!

**What you need**
- plastic box
- some modelling clay
- plastic toys, shells, etc.
- plaster of Paris
- water

## What to do

1. First, press the modelling clay into the bottom of your plastic bowl. It needs to be about 2–3 centimetres deep.

2. Next, push some small plastic toys (or anything else you want to turn into a fossil) into the modelling clay. Then remove the objects so you can see the impression left behind.

3. Mix some plaster of Paris with water, following the instructions on the packet. The mixture needs to be quite runny.

4. Pour the plaster of Paris into the bowl, over the modelling clay. It should be about 2 centimetres deep.

5. Let the plaster dry for 24 hours, then carefully take it out of the box. Finally, get rid of the modelling clay.

6. You can paint the plaster to look like a real fossil if you like. Your fossil is finished!

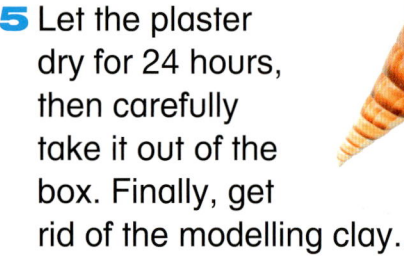

**2** Write the answers to the questions below.

   **a** Which text gives instructions? Find two features of an instruction text that this piece has.

   **b** How did you know that the other text was a report? Write two features of the report.

   **c** What's the best place to look for real fossils?

   **d** What is the most essential piece of kit for fossil hunting?

   **e** Why is it important for children to go fossil hunting with an adult?

   **f** Write the words and phrases in the report which the writer has used to grab the reader's attention.

   **g** Why do you think the report includes subheadings?

   **h** What do you use plaster of Paris for, if you want to make a fake fossil?

   **i** Do you leave the plastic toys in the clay, or take them out? Why?

   **j** Look at the section headed 'What to do'. Are most of the sentences statements, questions or orders? How do you know?

   **k** Why has the writer of the instruction text numbered the instructions and used bullet points?

   **l** How has the writer of the instruction text tried to grab the reader's attention?

   **m** How easy do you think it would be to follow the instructions? Could the writer have added anything to make it easier?

**3** Write out the sentences below. Add an appropriate connective in each gap.

   **a** I went down to the beach _____ jumped straight into the waves.

   **b** _____, I trod on a crab.

   **c** My toe went bright red, _____ the crab nipped it.

   **d** I showed my sister, _____ she just laughed at me.

   **e** _____, when I got home, my mother gave me a plaster for my sore toe.

### Connectives

The report and the instruction text use connectives in different ways.

- In the report, connectives are used to show how different ideas or statements are connected.
- In the instructions, connectives are used to show the order in which things happen.

# Writing

## Step 1: Planning

Plan and write two magazine articles of your own – a report and a set of instructions. You can base them on a hobby or sport you enjoy.

1. Think about your favourite hobby or sport. Share ideas with your partner about:
   - a good topic for a non-chronological report.
   - a good topic for a set of instructions.

2. Do some research if you need to, so that you know what you are going to say. You can use books or magazines about your hobby or sport, or use the internet. Make notes to remind you of the information you find out.

3. Write a rough draft of your report and your instructions.

## Step 2: Redrafting and revising

4. Read the drafts out loud to yourself. Think about these things:
   - Are your instructions clear and interesting to read?
   - Will your reader be able to follow them?
   - Is it clear what equipment your reader needs to follow the instructions?
   - Is your report interesting to read? Have you used language that grabs the reader's attention?
   - Have you used subheadings to help your reader?
   - Have you used connectives correctly?
   - Do all your sentences make sense?
   - Have you used punctuation correctly?
   - Are all your spellings correct?

5. Write a final version of both pieces, making any changes that you need to make. Remember to add some pictures.

### Thinking time

Do you think you should believe everything you read in newspaper and magazine articles? What could you do to check?

# 7 Inventions

## Reading and writing

**1** Read the text below from an encyclopedia of inventions. Then answer the questions.

> **Think!**
> Where would you find encyclopedias in the library?

# Encyclopedia of Inventions

### Ballpoint pen

Before the Hungarian inventor Laszlo Biro invented the ballpoint pen in 1938, people used fountain pens, which had to be filled with liquid ink. This took time, and the ink often made a mess. Biro's pen was quick, convenient and easy to use. Each ballpoint pen had ink stored inside it. The ink trickled slowly down over a ball at the tip of the pen. The ball rolled the ink on to the paper and made it easy to write smoothly and clearly.

Biro's invention is still very successful!

### Bicycle

The very first bicycle was invented in about 1790, in France. It was made of wood, and it had no pedals! The first pedal bicycle was invented in 1861 by the Michaux family, also in France. Since then, bicycles have changed a lot. Modern bicycles are much lighter and easier to ride than the early bicycles were.

## Cardigan

A cardigan is a type of sweater that has buttons down the front. It is named after a soldier, the 7th Earl of Cardigan in England, who wore a jacket like this in the 1850s.

## Fridge (Refrigerator)

The first working fridge was built by Jacob Perkins in 1834. Before that, it was very difficult to keep food cold – people used ice, but it melted easily. Perkins's invention made a big difference, but people still had to wait nearly 80 years for the first fridge that could be used at home, which was created in 1913.

## Sandwich

Sandwiches are often said to have been invented by an English man called John Montagu. He was the Earl of Sandwich, in the 18th century. He loved playing cards so much that he didn't want to stop for a proper meal. He asked his servants to bring him meat between two slices of bread, so he didn't have to pause his game to eat.

## Wellington boot

Nowadays, the name 'Wellington boot' or 'wellie' means waterproof boots made of plastic or rubber. But originally, Wellington boots were made of leather. They were made popular by a famous soldier, the Duke of Wellington, in about 1815.

## Windscreen wiper

The very first cars didn't have windscreen wipers, which meant it was quite dangerous to drive them in the rain – you wouldn't be able to see where you were going! Lots of people seem to have had the idea for windscreen wipers at about the same time. Among the people credited with inventing windscreen wipers in the early 1900s are Mary Anderson in the USA, and Gladstone Adams in England.

**2** **Write the answers to the questions below.**

a When was the ballpoint pen invented?

b How was Laszlo Biro's invention an improvement on what people had used before?

c Find two ways in which the very first bicycle was different from bicycles today.

d When was the first fridge that could be used in people's homes invented?

e Who was the sandwich named after and why?

f Look at the section headed 'Sandwich'. Write down the key words and phrases that show what this section is mostly about.

g Write one sentence to sum up the main point of the section headed 'Sandwich'.

h What were the first Wellington boots made of?

i Find two inventions that were named after soldiers.

j Why are windscreen wipers a good idea?

k How are the entries in this encyclopedia organised?

l Here are some new entries for the encyclopedia. Write out the list of entries (the headings) from the *Encyclopedia of Inventions* on page 75–76, including the new ones in the list below. Slot in the new entries in the correct alphabetical order.

- light bulb
- aeroplane
- scooter
- computer
- telephone
- microwave
- central heating
- battery
- washing machine
- wheelchair

**Spelling log**

Remember to add any interesting words to your spelling log.

## Alphabetical order

When we put things in alphabetical order, we look first at the first letter of the word:

**a**pple    **b**anana    **c**herry

Often, though, there is more than one word that starts with the same letter, so we need to look at the second letter of each word too:

a**p**ple    a**v**ocado    b**a**nana    b**r**ead    c**a**uliflower    c**h**erry

So 'cauliflower' comes before 'cherry' because *ca* comes before *ch*.

Sometimes there are words that start with the same two letters – so we need to look at the third letter:

ap**p**le    ap**r**icot

'Apple' comes first, because *p* comes before *r*.

Sometimes you have to look at a lot of letters!

ball**e**t    ball**g**ame    ball**p**ark

**3** Put the words below in alphabetical order.

> basketball   football   baseball   cricket   rugby   tennis
> table tennis   rounders   volleyball   badminton   squash

**4** Think of three more sports. Add their names to the list in the right places.

## Listening and speaking

**1** **PAIR WORK.** Reread *Encyclopedia of Inventions*. Talk about which of the inventions you think is the most important. Did you both choose the same invention?

- If so, share your ideas about what makes this invention important and make some notes about your reasons.
- If not, try to convince your partner that you are right. Remember to be polite and to listen to their views. Decide on one invention that you think is the most important. Make some notes about your reasons.

**2** **Write a list of the other inventions in *Encyclopedia of Inventions*. Put them in order, from most important to least important.**

- If you don't agree about the order at first, talk about it with your partner.
- Make some notes about why you chose your least important invention.

**3** **Use your notes to explain to the class why you chose your most and least important invention.**

## Writing

**1** **Use your notes to help you write a letter to a newspaper. Say why you think the invention you chose is very important. Remember:**

- Begin your letter 'Dear Sir or Madam'. Put your address and the date at the top.
- Start your letter with a sentence or paragraph that introduces the invention and says that it is very important.
- Put each of your reasons for thinking the invention is important in a separate paragraph.
- Remember to use connectives that help to explain your ideas. For example, 'because', 'in addition', 'therefore'.
- Finish with a paragraph that starts with the connective 'In conclusion'. This paragraph should sum up your views on why the invention is important.
- End your letter 'Yours faithfully,' and sign your name at the bottom.

*Apartment 17B*
*Harbour Heights*
*Hong Kong*

*17 November 2021*

*Dear Sir or Madam,*

**2** **Read your letter out loud to yourself to check that it makes sense.**

**3** **Make changes if you need to. Then write out a final version of your letter.**

## Reading and writing

**1** Read the poem below about an unusual invention. Then answer the questions.

### A Good Idea

**Glossary**

*gravy* a warm sauce you eat with meat and vegetables

*greengrocer* a person who sells fruit and vegetables

*truncheon* a short stick that a policeman carries

Today I might just make
one of my inventions.

What will you invent?

A machine to stand by the cooker
and stir the gravy.
Mum can have time off.

But who will do the vegetables?

This machine has another arm
which can peel potatoes,
chop them up
and put them in the pan.

But who will buy the potatoes?

This machine has another arm
with a basket on the end,
which stretches out of the door,
down the street
and into the greengrocer's shop.

But how does it pay the shopkeeper?

You put money in the basket,
he puts in potatoes.

But what if someone steals
the money?

This machine has another arm
with a policeman on the end,
carrying a truncheon.

Will it be ready by dinnertime?

No. Today I might just help Mum
to make the dinner myself.

by Irene Rawnsley

**2** Write the answers to the questions below.

a What does the invention in the poem do? Describe it in your own words.
b Where would the machine get the potatoes from?
c How would the machine pay for the potatoes?
d Why does the inventor include a policeman in the invention?
e Why does the inventor want to make a machine like this?
f Why does the inventor say 'Today I might just help Mum to make the dinner myself'?
g This poem is like a conversation. Write down one question from the poem and the answer to the question.
h Who do you think is talking in this poem?
i Do you think the inventor in this poem has ever made an invention before? Write down the line that gives you a clue about this.
j Do you think an invention like this could work? Why or why not?

## Using verb tenses

**1** The poem *A Good Idea* includes sentences in the present and future tenses. Find one sentence that uses the present and one that uses the future. Write them out.

**2** Write out the sentences below. Change the tenses.

a Change to future: I went into town with Mara and Jake.
b Change to present: Dad was cross with us.
c Change to future: Uncle Ike is making lamb curry for dinner.
d Change to past: My favourite TV show is *Dinosaur Wars*.
e Change to future: It was bedtime when we got to Gran's house.
f Change to present: Jamie ran home because it was raining.

## Punctuation

**1** The poet has deliberately left out all the end-of-sentence punctuation in this conversation poem. Write the poem out and add in the missing punctuation.

### I'm bored with walking to school

I'm bored with walking to school
Today I'm going to fly there

　　But where are your wings

Here they are, in my bag
They're a bit crumpled,
but they're not broken

　　How do they work

I just pull this string
and jump up into the air
as high as I can
Then I make a wish and –
look – I can fly

by Catherine Baker

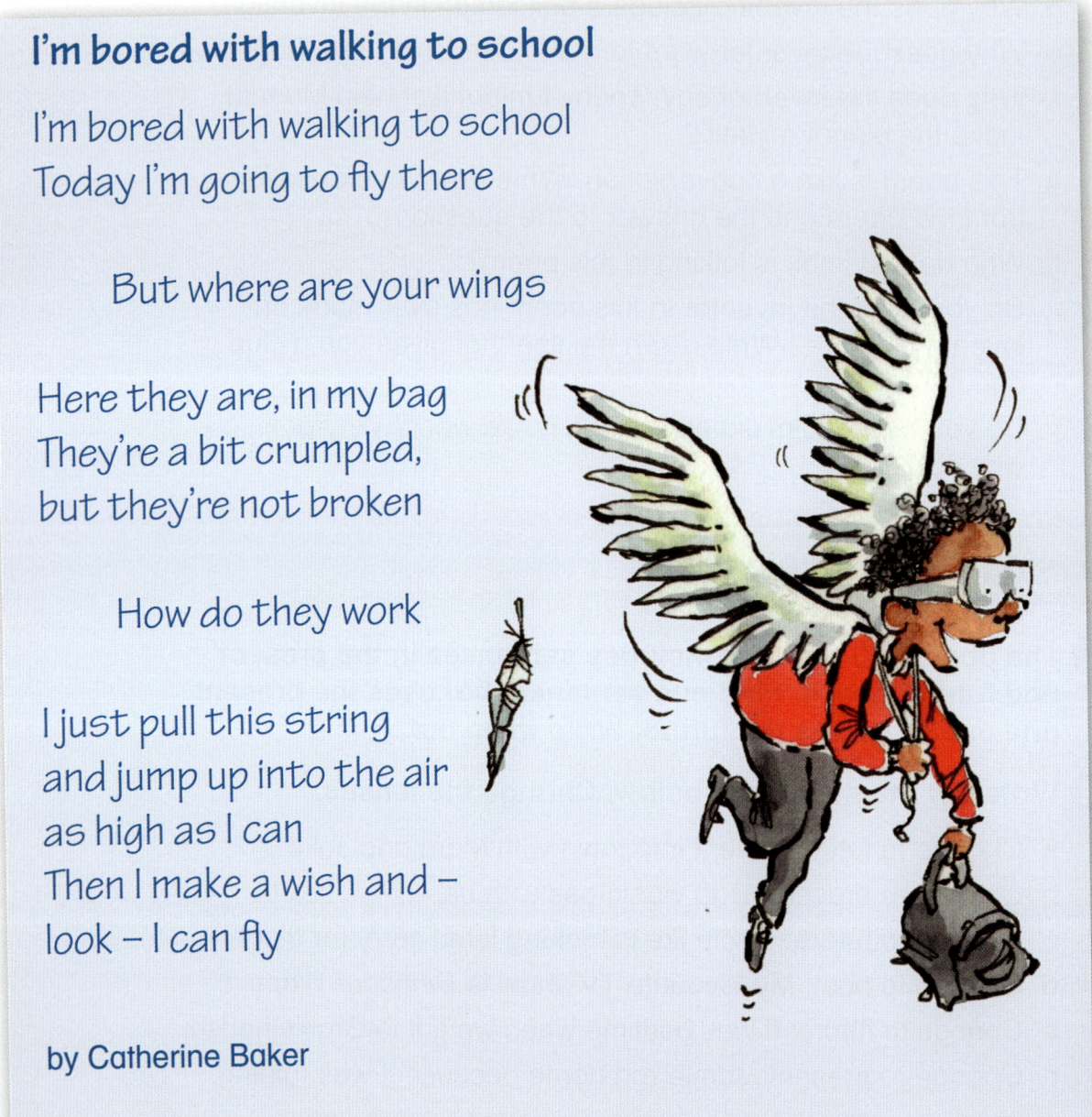

**2** PAIR WORK. Write a 'question and answer' conversation. Write at least two questions and two answers. Remember to use the right punctuation.

## Listening and speaking

1. Think of an idea for an invention you would like to make. It can be realistic or imaginary. Write some notes about it.

2. PAIR WORK. Tell your partner about your invention. They can ask you questions about it and you can make up the answers (but make them sound believable). Then swap and ask them about their invention.

3. Add more details to your notes. Use some of the ideas from your discussion.

## Writing

1. Write about your invention for the *Encyclopedia of Inventions.* Read the bullet points below. You will need to include these things in your writing.

   - what the invention is for
   - who invented it (you) and when (this year)
   - how the invention works
   - what is good about the invention

2. Use the bullet points as headings. Write some notes about your invention under each heading.

3. Use your notes and headings to help you write the Encyclopedia entry. Each heading can be a separate paragraph.

4. Read through your Encyclopedia entry. Check that your handwriting is clear and that your entry uses correct grammar, spelling and punctuation. Make changes if you need to.

5. Draw and label a diagram of your invention so the reader can see how it works.

## Reading and writing

**1** Read the information about reference texts. What is the purpose of a reference text?

**2** Now read the short explanation text below. Then answer the questions.

> **Reference texts**
>
> Reference texts give a specific kind of **information**. For example, a reader might use the *Encyclopedia of Inventions* if they want to find out how a particular thing was invented.
>
> Another kind of reference text is an **explanation**. Explanation texts tell the reader all about how something works, or why something happens.

# How do zips work?

You probably own at least one piece of clothing that has a zip fastener. Zips are very handy — they are easy to use, they work with any type of fabric, and they help to keep you warm.

The zip as we know it today was invented in about 1913 by Gideon Sundback, in the USA. Here's how this ingenious invention works!

- Each side of the zip fastener has rounded 'teeth'.
- The teeth on one side of the zip fit into the gaps on the other side of the zip.
- When you pull the metal slider up the zip, the slider forces the two rows of teeth together.
- This closes the zip securely.
- When you want to undo the zip, you just use the slider to separate the teeth again.

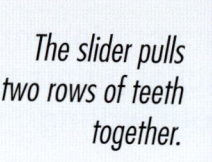

*The slider pulls two rows of teeth together.*

**3** Write the answers to the questions below.

a Explain in your own words what the 'teeth' of a zip are.
b Find and write down a word from the text that means the same as 'clever'.
c What does the slider on a zip do?
d Why do you think the writer used bullet points in this explanation text?
e Which tense is this text mostly written in? Why do you think the writer used this tense?
f Why do you think the writer included a diagram?

## Writing

1. **Look at the diagram. Which invention from the *Encyclopedia of Inventions* (pages 75–76) does it go with?**

2. **Use information from the diagram and from the *Encyclopedia of Inventions* to help you write a short explanation of how a ballpoint pen works.**

   Remember to:
   - introduce the explanation by telling the reader something about ballpoint pens.
   - use bullet points to separate out the different parts of your explanation.
   - use short sentences in the present tense.

## Spelling

Look at the noun 'explanation'. It comes from the verb 'to explain'. Nouns that come from verbs usually end in either *–ion* or *–ment*.

1. **Write the verb that each of the nouns below comes from.**

   > invention   action
   > imagination   movement
   > judgement

2. **Write some other nouns you can think of which end in *–ion* or *–ment* and the verbs they come from.**

### Thinking deeper

How many nouns can you make in a word family? Play a game and find out.

Work in teams. Your teacher will give you a set of word cards. Take turns to choose a word and make a noun in the same word family by adding an ending. You have 30 seconds to make and spell the word correctly.

# Writing

## Step 1: Planning

**1** Velcro® is a special sort of fastening that is used on clothes. Look at these short notes, pictures and diagrams which show how it was invented and how it works.

### Velcro®
- Invented by George de Mestral in Switzerland, 1948.
- He went for a walk with his dog. Noticed that seeds and burrs from plants got stuck in the dog's fur.
- The seeds and burrs had hooks that helped them to cling on to the dog's fur.
- Took 8 years of research until George got the design right.

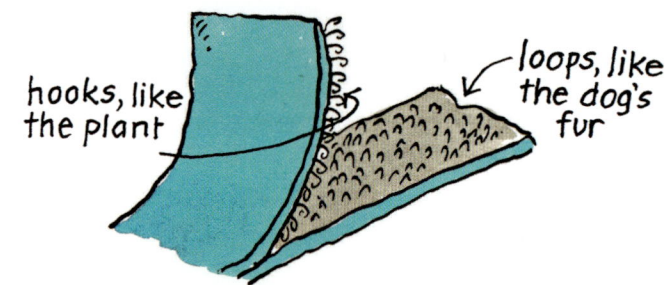

**2** Take turns with your partner to explain in your own words how Velcro® was invented and how it works.

**3** Write some notes under these headings.
- What Velcro® is used for
- How George de Mestral got the idea
- How George created Velcro®
- How Velcro® works

**4** Write a rough draft of an explanation about Velcro®. Use your notes and the headings.

## Step 2: Redrafting and revising

**1** Read your explanation out loud to yourself. Check it for sense. Also check your spelling and grammar.

**2** Write a final version of your explanation and diagram. Make any changes you need to.

### Thinking time

Did you find it easy or difficult to write an explanation of how something works? Give a reason for your answer.

# 8 Putting on a show

**Listening and speaking**

**PAIR WORK.**

**1** **Listen as your teacher reads you a summary of the story *Peter and the Wolf*. Write some notes to help you remember the main things that happen in the story.**

**2** **Take turns to retell the story.**

- You don't need to include every detail, but try to remember all the most important parts.
- When it is your turn to listen, help your partner remember any important parts they have forgotten.

**3** **How do you think the wolf felt at the end of the story? Decide who will play the part of the wolf and who will play the part of a TV reporter.**

**The TV reporter interviews the wolf and asks him:**

- how he feels about what has happened.
- what he thinks about Peter.
- what he hopes to do in the future.

87

## Reading and writing

> **Playscripts**
> Playscripts:
> - have character names in the margin followed by the words they say.
> - include stage directions.
> - are organised in sections called acts and scenes.

**1** Read the playscript version of part of the story of *Peter and the Wolf* below. Then answer the questions.

# Peter and the Wolf

Peter and his grandfather live in the middle of a forest. There is a meadow just in front of their cottage, but Grandfather won't let Peter play there, because of the dangerous wolf who lives in the forest. But Peter disobeys Grandfather. When Grandfather finds Peter playing in the meadow, he is angry and sends Peter to his room. Peter's friends Duck, Cat and Bird are still in the meadow.

### Scene 3: The Edge of the Forest

**NARRATOR:** As soon as Peter and Grandfather had gone, a big, grey wolf came creeping out of the forest.

**WOLF:** Ha ha ha! Peter's gone. Now I can catch my dinner!

*(The wolf prowls up to Cat.)*

**CAT:** *(jumping into the tree)* MIAOW! MIAOOOOW!

**NARRATOR:** The wolf ran over to the pond. Duck saw the wolf, so she waddled out of the pond and tried to run away through the forest.

**DUCK:** QUACK! QUACK!

**WOLF:** Yummy! Duck dinner for me!

*(Duck runs away from the wolf, but he catches up with her.)*

**NARRATOR:** With one big gulp, the wolf swallowed Duck up whole.

**WOLF:** GULP! Slurp! Slobber!

**NARRATOR:** High up in the tree, Cat and Bird looked down at the wolf. The wolf looked up at them.

**WOLF:** *(licking his lips)* Yoo-hoo! I'm coming to get you, too.

**NARRATOR:** But Peter had seen everything. He climbed out of his bedroom window and ran over to the tree, carrying a strong rope.

| | |
|---|---|
| **PETER:** | *(whispering to himself)* I'm going to teach that wicked wolf a lesson. |

*(Peter scrambles up the tree where Bird and Cat are sitting.)*

| | |
|---|---|
| **PETER:** | *(quietly)* Bird, go and fly around the wolf's head. |
| **BIRD:** | TWEEEET! No, he'll eat me! |
| **PETER:** | Trust me! You must fly around the wolf, till he's sick and dizzy. And keep him near the bottom of the tree! |
| **BIRD:** | *(flying round the wolf's head)* WHEEEEE! |
| **WOLF:** | Oi! Silly Bird. Go away. You're making me dizzy. |

*(Peter makes a lasso out of the rope, and dangles it down until it slips over the wolf's tail.)*

| | |
|---|---|
| **NARRATOR:** | The wolf didn't see Peter ... but he felt the lasso when it was pulled tight around his tail. |
| **WOLF:** | OWW! What's that? Get off my tail! |

*(Peter ties the end of the rope round the thick branch where he, Cat and Bird are sitting.)*

| | |
|---|---|
| **PETER:** | Ha ha! I've got you, you big, bad wolf. |
| **NARRATOR:** | Just then, a hunter plodded out of the forest. |
| **HUNTER:** | Aha! A bird! I think I'll shoot it! |
| **PETER:** | No! Don't shoot! Bird and I have caught the big, bad wolf. |
| **HUNTER:** | Amazing! Let's take him to the zoo. |

## Scene 4: On the Way to the Zoo

| | |
|---|---|
| **NARRATOR:** | Peter skipped all the way to the zoo, followed by the hunter with the wolf. Grandfather and Cat came along too. Overhead, Bird chirped merrily. |
| **GRANDFATHER:** | You're a brave boy, Peter. I'm not cross with you any more. |
| **BIRD:** | Tweet, tweet! Peter is the bravest boy in the world! |
| **DUCK:** | *(very quietly, from inside the wolf's stomach)* Quack! Quack! Quack! |

**2** Write the answers to the questions below.

a Why didn't Grandfather want Peter to play in the meadow?
b What punishment does Peter get for disobeying Grandfather?
c What does the wolf have for his dinner?
d What does Peter use the rope for?
e What does Bird do to help Peter catch the wolf?
f Why isn't Grandfather cross with Peter in the end?
g Why do you think the words in brackets are included in the playscript?
h Why are some of the words that the characters say written in capitals?
i Write a paragraph to describe Peter. Include what he looks like, what he does and what kind of person he is.
j What do you think will happen to the duck? Write at least three sentences about what you think will happen next.

### Thinking deeper

Work in groups. Think about the scene you listened to and then read aloud.
- Which version do you prefer? Give a reason for your answer.
- Is a play easier or more difficult to understand than a told story?
- Why do you think actors in plays need stage instructions, props and sometimes a narrator?

## Using verb tenses

**1** Write a list of all the verbs in the playscript that describe the different ways the characters move.

**2** PAIR WORK. Take turns to act out moving in the way each verb describes.

**3** Look at the tenses of the verbs you listed. Write 'past' or 'present' by each verb.

**4** Which tense appears most often in the speeches? Why do you think that is?

**5** Why do you think the Narrator's speeches use the past tense?

## Reading and writing

**1** Below is a text from *Zlata's Diary* and on page 92 is the start of a playscript based on this diary entry. Read them both. Then answer the questions.

The diary was kept by a young girl, Zlata Filipovic, during the Bosnian War in the early 1990s. Zlata lived in the city of Sarajevo, which was bombed a lot during the war. She called her diary Mimmy!

**Remember!**
Use your knowledge of punctuation to help you read and understand the text clearly.

### Thursday, 6 May 1993

Dear Mimmy,

Today – drama in the house.

I was sitting in the room, reading, when suddenly something darted across the floor. And you know what it was, Mimmy? A tiny little mouse. So small that I barely recognised it for what it was. He ran under the built-in bookcase in the niche by the wall. Mummy screamed. She climbed on to a chair and then ran off into my room. I know she would have liked to run out of the house, but … THERE'S A WAR ON.

What to do? We had to catch it. But how? I ran off to get Cici (cats are mouse specialists), and Daddy and Braco reached for their tools, screwdrivers and things. They took down the bookcase. Cici was waiting in ambush. Daddy and Braco took down the shelves and I took down the books. And Mummy? She was in my room waiting, of course. When they removed the bookcase they found a little hole in the wall where he had escaped. They blocked off the hole with plaster, put everything back and tried to persuade Mummy to come back in and move around the house normally.

We tried to convince her, but she was all in knots. We moved Cici in with us. Now she sleeps in our flat and Mummy feels a bit safer (I hope). The mouse has run away and probably won't come back. Mummy doesn't believe it, though.

Just when we thought we had resolved the problem of the mouse, he began to scratch at the wall again. He wanted to get back in. He's really silly. Doesn't he realise that we're trying to get rid of him? He's an animal, after all, Mimmy.

Mummy is going out of her mind. I have to do something about that mouse. I'm going to talk to Cici and have her fix things.

Ciao!

Zlata

**SCENE:** In a living room with chairs, sofa and a built-in bookcase. DADDY and MUMMY are sitting on the sofa; MUMMY is knitting and DADDY is reading a book. ZLATA is also reading a book, lying on her stomach on a rug. The scene is peaceful. Suddenly a tiny mouse runs across the floor.

ZLATA: (*suddenly lifting her head*) Oh! What's that?
MUMMY: (*distractedly, not looking up*) I don't know, Zlata.
ZLATA: Oh, my goodness! It's a mouse! Such a little one – how cute!
MUMMY: (*standing up in a panic*) Aaargh! A mouse! Help!

(*The mouse disappears under the bookcase*)

DADDY: (*calmly*) Don't panic, dear. It's just a mouse – it can't hurt you!
MUMMY: (*climbing up on a chair*) I don't care! I hate mice!

**2** Write the answers to the questions below about the diary entry.

  a  Where did the mouse run to hide?
  b  Why couldn't Mummy run out of the house?
  c  Who is Cici?
  d  What did Zlata do to help solve the mouse problem?
  e  Explain in your own words what the phrases below from the diary entry mean.
   • 'waiting in ambush'
   • 'all in knots'
   • 'going out of her mind'

**3** Write *at least four* differences between the diary and the playscript.

  a  Think about:
   • which tells us most about what the characters said and did.
   • which tells us most about what the characters felt.
   • differences in the ways the two texts are written and organised.
   • things that are in one text but not the other and why.
  b  How do you think the playscript version might help the actor playing Mummy?

## Writing

**Writing a playscript**
- Start each new speech by putting the character's name in capital letters in the margin.
- Don't use speech marks – just write the words the characters say.

**1** **Read the information above about writing a playscript.**

Write a short playscript scene where Daddy and Zlata try to persuade Mummy to come back into the living room, but Mummy is too scared. Base it on information from Zlata's diary, but make up what the characters say and how they say it. Start like this:

ZLATA: (*cheerfully*) It's OK, Mummy! You can come back in now!

**2** **PAIR WORK. When you have finished, read your playscript aloud to your partner.**

- Does it sound good?
- Is there anything you could change to make it better?

## Listening and speaking

**GROUP WORK.**

**1** **Take a role each: Zlata, Daddy and Mummy. Imagine that you think the mouse has gone, but you suddenly hear it scratching at the wall again.**

- Think about what your character might say about the situation.
- What would your character do next? Make some quick notes to help you remember.

**2** Act out the situation. Try to make your acting as realistic as possible.

**3** Your scene should last about three minutes.

- When you have finished, think about what went well and what you would like to change.
- Practise again, before showing your scene to the rest of the class.

### Remember!
- Think about how your character would feel and what they would say or do – act like your character, not like yourself.
- Listen to what the other characters say and respond to them. You might not be able to use all of your notes.

## Spelling

**1** Read the spelling rules. Then add *in–*, *im–*, *ir–* or *il–* to the root words below to give them the opposite meaning.

> human    logical    mortal    sane    polite
> convenient    rational    audible

### SPELLING RULES: *im–*, *ir–* or *il–* ?

- Add *in*, in front of *most* root words to change them to their opposite: '**in**correct', '**in**efficient', '**in**visible'.
- If the root word begins with *m* or *p*, then add *im–* to the root word: '**im**perfect', '**im**mobile'.
- If the root word begins with *r*, add *ir–* to the root word: '**ir**regular'.
- If the root word begins with *l*, add *il–* to the root word: '**il**legal'.

### Prefixes
The prefixes *in–*, *im–*, *ir–*, or *il–* change the meaning of a root word to its opposite:

- 'in' + root word 'credible' = 'incredible' (not 'credible')
- 'im' + root word 'possible' = 'impossible' (not 'possible')
- 'ir' + root word 'regular' = 'irregular' (not 'regular')
- 'il' + root word 'legal' = 'illegal' (not 'legal')

**2** Read the spelling rules. Then make the words below plural.

cat   book   shelf   bush   elf
baby   watch   lady   box
fly   mess   telephone

**Spelling log**

Record interesting words in your spelling log.

### SPELLING RULES: forming plurals

If you want to turn a singular noun into a plural, you usually add –s at the end, like this:
  things   knots   rugs

Some nouns change spelling when you make them plural.

- Nouns ending in –y change to end in –ies:
  welly/wellies   worry/worries   jelly/jellies

- Nouns ending in –f often change to end in –ves:
  loaf/loaves   calf/calves

- Nouns ending in –ss, –ch, –sh and –x change to end in –es:
  kiss/kisses   lunch/lunches   flash/flashes   fox/foxes

**3** Think of one plural noun with each of the endings –s, –ies, –ves and –es. Write a sentence using each of your plural nouns.

### Writing

Write a playscript about a difficult problem. First you are going to plan it. Then you are going to write it out.

## Step 1: Planning

**1** Think of a difficult problem to write about. It can be something that has happened to you or to someone you know, or it can be something you have read or heard about. If you prefer, you could use one of these ideas:

- There's a new child at school who is a bit different from everyone else. Some children start picking on the new child. You think this is unfair, but you don't want the others to start teasing you too. What could you do?
- You have seen a friend of yours taking food from someone else's lunchbox. When the teacher asks who did it, your friend says it wasn't him. What could you do?
- You've been asked to donate some toys as gifts for sick children who are in hospital. Your mother suggests that you give away one of your favourite toys, but you don't want to. What could you do?

**2** Now write some quick notes about your idea.

**3** Talk to your partner about your ideas. Tell them the outline of the situation. Then have a go at acting out the conversation in a group.

**4** Use your notes and ideas from your acting to help you write a first draft of your dialogue.

## Step 2: Redrafting and revising

**5** In your group, act out the scene using your first draft dialogue. Does it sound good? What could you change to make it even better?

**6** Write a final draft of your dialogue.

**7** When you are happy with your dialogue, act it out again with your group. Maybe you will get the chance to perform it for other people, too.

### Thinking time

What have you learned about dealing with difficult problems from the diary and play in this unit?

# 9 Imaginary worlds

## Listening and speaking

**1** Listen as your teacher reads you the first part of a story called *Sheetal's First Landing*. This is a fantasy story.

**2** Listen to the story again. Think about what might happen next. Make some notes about:

- what the tomb might be like.
- what Sheetal might see and hear.
- how Sheetal might feel.
- who else might be in this part of the story.
- what might happen.

**3** PAIR WORK. Talk about your ideas. Decide what you both think is most likely to happen. Share your ideas with the rest of the class.

> **Fantasy stories**
> Fantasy stories:
> - are stories about people, creatures and places that are not real.
> - take place in an imaginary world.

97

## Reading and writing

**1** Look at the pictures and skim the rest of the story you have listened to. Note the main events of the story. Then read the story again slowly.

# Sheetal's First Landing

*Sheetal has grown up on a huge spaceship that explores the galaxy. Now her help is needed to investigate a mysterious alien planet.*

I looked around at the strange alien desert of blue-white sand. On the horizon, a dark, evil smudge of clouds flickered with lightning. It was the storm we'd been warned about, approaching fast. In front of me was the alien tomb we'd come to study – a vast, solid, oval bunker. My mother waved from the roof of the tomb. The only way into the tomb was through a hole in the roof, near where Mum was standing.

I clipped a rope to my suit harness and was winched up.

"Happy birthday, sweetie!" Mum said. She sounded exhausted – they'd all been working flat out for days. "Be careful – this tomb roof is mostly made of trap-doors. Goodness knows what the alien builders were thinking. That rainstorm's going to open the trap-doors, then flood the whole tomb!"

My job was to winch down into the tomb to attach sensors inside. Mum said, "You OK?" Maybe she was worried about me.

"Yes, Mum," I said. (Really! I was *qualified* for this!) "I'll talk all the time I'm down there, so you know I'm OK. I'll position the sensors. Routine stuff."

Mum patted my shoulder. "Sounds good. Ready?"

I nodded, and began talking.

"Sheetal Lin-Evans lowering into the Alien Tomb.

The sun's shining through the roof hatch like a spotlight, but otherwise it's utterly dark. But that's OK – my suit lights are on. The tomb is packed with big things like cocoons, hanging from the roof on ropes. It's OK – I'm small enough to squeeze past. I'm positioning the first sensor. Now I'm winching down to position the second sensor …"

I went on winching slowly down the wall of the tomb, attaching sensors, talking all the time. Just keep talking, I told myself. Sound calm and be calm. It wasn't really spooky – not spooky, but *amazing!* The cocoon things were the mummified bodies of real aliens, frog-like creatures who built the tomb ages ago. And they'd made wall paintings! I could see pictures showing that this desert was covered in lakes long ago. Then the pictures showed dead aliens being wrapped up, and hoisted into this tomb in the sand. The last pictures showed lakes and live aliens again. The Alien Afterlife perhaps – who could tell?

I stood on the floor of the tomb to fix the last sensor. Maybe no human had ever stood there before – or ever would do again. I wrote 'S L-E 9' in the sand with my finger. Then I winched up.

We climbed down the outside of the tomb. You could actually hear the storm coming now– the distant rain sounded like someone raking gravel. Raindrops began to fall on us as we reached the ship. Then it was as if giants were hurling buckets of water everywhere. So this was what *weather* was like.

When we got back into orbit, we checked the sensor camera. We could see the tomb flooding. Then there was nothing except muddy, swirling water. ("Alien mummy soup – yuck!" Dad said.) But then we saw something moving! I actually screamed. In the murky water I saw live aliens, freeing themselves from the cocoons.

Then an alien hand reached out, and grabbed the sensor.

The End [?]

**2** **PAIR WORK. Talk about the questions below. Then write the answers.**

   a  How does Sheetal get down into the alien tomb?

   b  Why does Sheetal need to keep talking all the time that she's in the tomb?

   c  Find a clue (in the paragraph that starts 'I went on winching') that helps us to guess that the aliens might be coming alive at the end of the story. Explain what the clue means in your own words.

   d  Why do you think Sheetal writes 'S L-E 9' on the floor of the tomb?

   e  Whose viewpoint is the story told from?

   f  Find a simile in the story. What is it describing?

   g  Find one sentence of dialogue that is in the present tense and one sentence that is in the future. Remember to use speech marks when you write them.

   h  What clues can you find that tell you this is a science-fiction story?

**3** Write a paragraph to describe the inside of the tomb. Include adjectives and phrases to help the reader to 'see' it.

**4** Write three sentences to sum up the main things that happen in this story.

## Thinking deeper

How did Sheetal feel when she landed? Write down five words to describe this. Then use your words to make a very short poem about the experience.

## Listening and speaking

**1** PAIR WORK. Take turns to retell the story in your own words. Remind each other if you forget any important bits.

**2** GROUP WORK. Talk about what might happen next in the story. Is it really the end?
- Talk about your ideas and agree on a good follow-up story.
- Act out the story in your group. Make sure everyone has a part.

### Story structure

You've already seen that many stories have five stages:

   introduction → build-up → climax → resolution → conclusion.

We can also show this as a 'story mountain'.

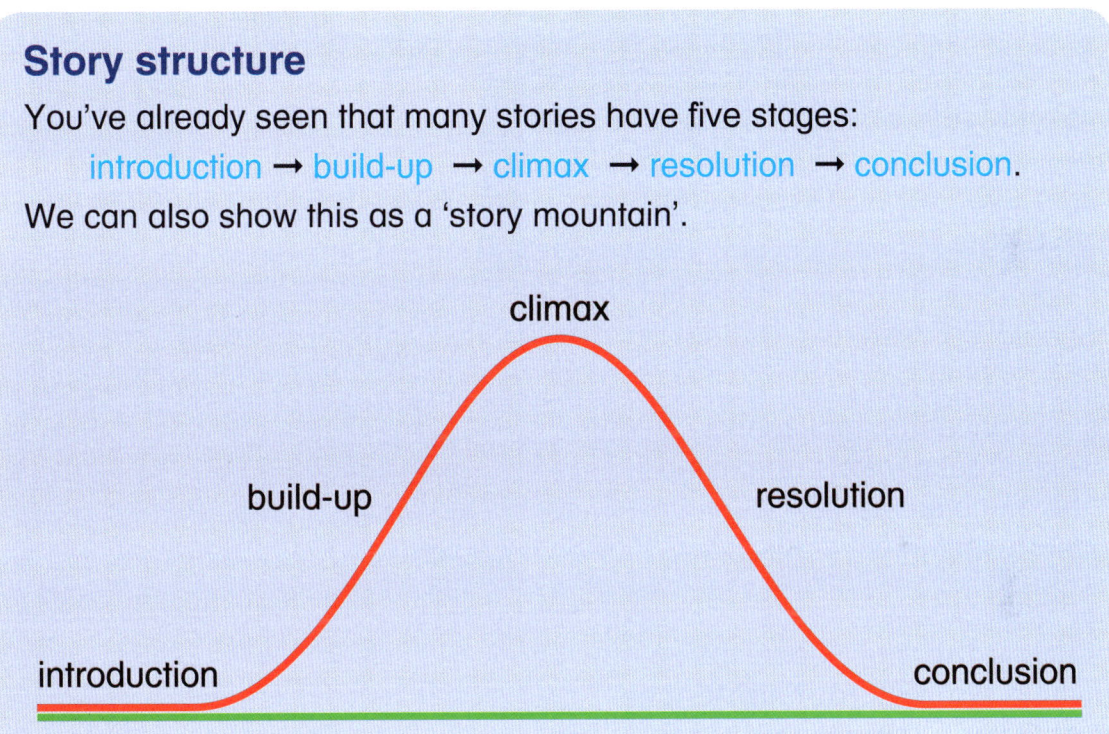

**3** Think about the story you acted out in your group.
- Does it fit the five stage pattern?
   introduction → build-up → climax → resolution → conclusion
- If not, how could you change it so that it follows the pattern?
- Act it out again.

## Reading and writing

### Story language

Writers often use expressive and descriptive language when they want to help the reader to imagine:
- the setting of the story.
- the atmosphere of the story (spooky, funny, sad ...).
- how the main characters feel.

1. **Find and write out a sentence from *Sheetal's First Landing* that uses expressive language in each of the ways below.**

   a  a sentence that describes what Sheetal can see, feel or hear (the 'setting')

   b  a sentence that makes the reader feel nervous or excited (the 'atmosphere')

   c  a sentence that describes how Sheetal feels

2. **Underline the most descriptive words in each of your sentences. Label them to show whether they are nouns, verbs, adjectives or adverbs.**

3. **Now write three more sentences of your own to describe the setting, the atmosphere and how Sheetal felt in the story. Can you make yours even more descriptive than the writer's?**

### Spelling log

Add interesting words to your spelling log.

## Reading

PAIR WORK. Here are two poems about imaginary animals. Read them twice – once silently to yourself and once out loud to your partner.

### Lost Magic

Today I found some lost magic –
a twisty-twirly horn
of a unicorn lying at my feet.
And when I stopped
to pick it up, to hold it
in my fist, I remembered
how once upon a time
you could always find unicorns,
but there are no unicorns now.

You would find them on the shoreline,
flitting in and out of caves in cliffs,
or climbing hills at twilight.
They would lead you through forests,
sometimes hiding behind trees,
and if you lost them or they lost you,
you could always find them again,
but there are no unicorns now.

And it didn't matter
if you followed them all day,
the edge of the world was miles away,
there was nothing to fear.
And none of the unicorns we knew ever
changed into dangerous strangers.

Once upon a time there were unicorns,
but there are no unicorns now.

by Brian Moses

### THE LAST DRAGON

By a dusk-damp cave
as the first snows fall
a dragon breathes;
the last of them all.

His eyes are dull,
his memories old;
his breath is pale,
his fire now cold.

The forest mice
who ran from his roar
now nest by his feet,
afraid no more.

He turns his face
to the winter moon;
his claws are furled,
his courage gone.

The first owl swoops
to the forest floor;
but the last of the dragons
is no more.

by Judith Nicholls

## Comprehension

**Write the answers to the questions below.**

a Where is *The Last Dragon* set? Write down three phrases from the poem that give you clues about the setting.

b What do you think 'dusk-damp' means? Explain it in your own words.

c What do the mice do that proves they are not afraid? Why aren't they afraid?

d Write down two pairs of rhyming words from *The Last Dragon*.

e One of the verses in *The Last Dragon* doesn't rhyme in the same way as the others. Which verse is this?

f In the line 'his claws are furled', what does 'furled' mean? Use a dictionary to help you if you need to.

g How does *The Last Dragon* make you feel? What would you say to the dragon if you could talk to him?

h In *Lost Magic*, what makes the narrator suddenly think about unicorns?

i Write down a repeating line from *Lost Magic*. Why do you think the writer repeats this line in the poem?

j How do you think the narrator of *Lost Magic* feels about the fact that there aren't any unicorns anymore?

k In what way are the poems similar. In what way are they different?

l Which of the poems do you prefer? Give at least two reasons for your choice.

### Thinking deeper

- *Lost Magic* is a very thoughtful poem. Sometimes in poems, one thing stands for something else. For example, a poet might write about a terrible storm and the storm might stand for the poet's feelings of anger, fear or sadness.

- In this poem, perhaps the unicorns stand for something else. What do you think they might stand for? There's no right or wrong answer to this, but be prepared to explain your reasons.

## Reading and writing

1. Reread *The Last Dragon* (page 103). Find all the words and phrases that describe the setting. Write them down.

2. PAIR WORK. Describe the setting out loud. Use words and phrases from the poem and add some descriptive words and phrases of your own.

3. Add your new words and phrases to the notes you made in question 1.

4. Now use your notes to help you write a detailed description of the setting.

5. Write a final draft of your description and add a picture.

### Remember!
Look at the words you have recorded in your spelling log and use them in your writing if you can.

# Reading

## Rhyming words

Poems like *The Last Dragon* contain lots of different kinds of rhyming words.

Some rhyming words use the same spelling patterns — like 'fall' and 'all'.

Others use different spelling patterns to make the same sound — like 'roar' and 'more'.

1. Write the rhyming words from *The Last Dragon*. Underline the parts of the words that rhyme.

2. Write the words with the same spelling patterns in lists.

3. Look at the spelling patterns in the words you have on your lists. Add two more rhyming words to each list.

4. PAIR WORK. Practise spelling the words on your lists. Then ask your partner to test you.

5. Choose one word from each of your lists and write a sentence that uses that word.

### Writing

Write your own fantasy story. Use one of the pictures below for an idea. You will need to make a plan first.

## Step 1: Planning

**1** Think about what might happen in the story. Write some notes to help you remember your ideas and then tell your partner about it. Can your partner help you improve your ideas so that your story sounds really exciting?

**2** Think about how your story will fit the five-stage story structure.
introduction → build-up → climax → resolution → conclusion

**3** Use the five story stages as headings and write notes about what happens under each heading. You could use the story mountain (page 101) to help you plan your story if you prefer.

**4** Use your plan to help you write your story. Each part of the plan will need *at least* one paragraph.

## Step 2: Redrafting and revising

**5** Read your first draft out loud to yourself and make changes if you need to.

**6** Now read the story out loud to your partner. Can they make any suggestions to improve the story?

**7** Write a final version of your story. Include all the changes that you think will improve it. Remember to include a picture that shows the main setting and any fantasy creatures.

**Text acknowledgements**

The publishers gratefully acknowledge the permissions granted to reproduce copyright material in the book. Every effort has been made to contact the holders of copyright material, but if any have been inadvertently overlooked, the Publisher will be pleased to make the necessary arrangements at the first opportunity.

Cover illustration: *The Brave Baby* Reprinted by permission of HarperCollins*Publishers* Ltd © 2004 Malachy Doyle, illustrated by Richard Johnson. *Let's Go To Mars* Reprinted by permission of HarperCollins*Publishers* Ltd © 2005 Janice Marriott, illustrated by Mark Ruffle; *The Brave Baby* Reprinted by permission of HarperCollins*Publishers* Ltd © 2004 Malachy Doyle, illustrated by Richard Johnson; *I've Just Had a Bright Idea!* Reprinted by permission of HarperCollins*Publishers* Ltd © 2010 Scoular Anderson; *Peter and the Wolf* Reprinted by permission of HarperCollins*Publishers* Ltd © 2007 Diane Redmond, illustrated by John Bendall-Brunello.

We are grateful to the following for permission to reproduce copyright material:
An extract on pp.2–3 from "Street Child" by Berlie Doherty published in *Collins Primary Literacy Pupil Book 4*, pp.4–5. Reproduced with permission of David Higham Associates; An extract on pp.31–32 adapted from *Collins Primary Literacy Pupil Book 4* by Ann Webley, pp.50–51, 90. Reproduced with permission of the author; The poem on p.51 'The Youngest' by Michael Rosen, published in *Mustard, Custard, Grumble Belly and Gravy*, Bloomsbury Publishing Plc. Reproduced by permission of Bloomsbury Publishing Ltd, and Peters Fraser & Dunlop on behalf of Michael Rosen; An extract on pp.53–54 from *Goggle Eyes* by Anne Fine, Penguin, copyright © Anne Fine, 1989. Reproduced with permission of David Higham Associates; The poem on p.57 'Eleven Years Old' from *Earth Magic* by Dionne Brand and illustrations by Eugenie Fernandes, text copyright © 1979, 2006 Dionne Brand. Reproduced by permission of Kids Can Press Ltd., Toronto, Canada; An extract on p.60 from "The New Boy" by Jamila Gavin published in *Kamla and Kate*, Egmont. Reproduced with permission of David Higham Associates; Extracts on pp.63, 67 from 'Malala's Award' and 'Mini Mars Mission'. Reproduced with permission of First News; The poem on p.80 "A Good Idea" by Irene Rawnsley published in *Dog's Dinner* by Irene Rawnsley, Methuen Children's Books, 1990. Reproduced by kind permission of the author; Extracts on pp.91, 92 from *Zlata's Diary: A child's life in Sarajevo* by Zlata Filipovic, translated by Christina Pribichevich-Zoric, translated by Christina Pribichevich-Zoric, Puffin, copyright © Fixot et editions Robert Faffont, 1993; translation copyright © Fixot et Editions Robert Laffont, 1994. Reproduced with permission from Penguin Books Limited and Viking Books, an imprint of Penguin Publishing Group, a division of Penguin Random House LLC. All rights reserved; An extract on pp.98–99 from *Sheetal's First Landing* by Chris Baker, copyright © Chris Baker, 2015. Reproduced by kind permission of the author; The poem on p.103 "The Last Dragon" by Judith Nicholls, published in *Storm's Eye*, Oxford University Press, 1994, copyright © Judith Nicholls, 1994. Reproduced by kind permission of the author; and the poem on p.103 "Lost Magic" by Brian Moses, published in *Behind the Staffroom Door*, Macmillan Children's Books, 2007. Reproduced by kind permission of the author.

In some instances we have been unable to trace the owners of copyright material, and we would appreciate any information that would enable us to do so.

**Photo acknowledgements**
The publishers wish to thank the following for permission to reproduce photographs. Every effort has been made to trace copyright holders and to obtain their permission for the use of copyright materials. The publishers will gladly receive any information enabling them to rectify any error or omission at the first opportunity.

(t = top, c = centre, b = bottom, r = right, l = left)

p1t World History Archive/Alamy Stock Photo, p2b dotshock/Shutterstock, p8 Old Paper Studios/Alamy, p12 Darrin Henry/Shutterstock, p13t Kummeleon/Shutterstock, p13b esfera/Shutterstock, p16 Samuel Borges Photography/Shutterstock, p19 Independent Picture Service/Alamy Stock Photo, p21 muratart/Shutterstock, p22 Science Photo Library – ANDRZEJ WOJCICKI/Getty Images, p23 Naturesauraphoto/Shutterstock, p25 Shaiith/Shutterstock, p26l Iakov Kalinin/Shutterstock, p26r Alexey U/Shutterstock, p27tr Andrey Yurlov/Shutterstock, p27bl muratart/Shutterstock, p27br Robert Daly/Getty Images, p29 Shutterstock, p30tl Jiri Foltyn/Shutterstock, p30tr Matthew Dixon/Shutterstock, p30b Doug Steakley/Getty Images, p32 Jim Holmes/Design Pics/Getty Images, p38 Monkey Business Images/Shutterstock, p39 Frances Linzee Gordon/Getty Images, p41 Eric Isselee/Shutterstock, p48 Alberto Loyo/Shutterstock, p52 glenda/Shutterstock, p56 Pawika Tongtavee/Shutterstock, p57 Nevskii Dmitrii/Shutterstock, p63 JStone/Shutterstock, p66 Eric Isselee/Shutterstock, p67 SergeyDV/Shutterstock, p68 Rashevska Nataliia/Shutterstock, p70l Paul Treadway/Alamy Stock Photo, p70tr CHARLOTTE GEKIERE/Getty Images, p70br MI News & Sport/Alamy Stock Photo, p71 Jim Wileman/Alamy Stock Photo, p72tr Lucie Lang/Shutterstock, p72bl Elena Ray/Shutterstock, p72bc Africa Studio/Shutterstock, p72br Alice-Photo/Shutterstock, p77 Science & Society Picture Library/Getty Images, p91 Rudmer Zwerver/Shutterstock, p93 Sinelev/Shutterstock, p102 Johan Swanepoel/Shutterstock.